Star
Sensational TUNA

One Fish Story
THAT'S WORTH A LISTEN

For centuries, people the world over have enjoyed a food that is convenient, versatile, satisfying, and nearly universally loved for its good taste. Its history is so unusual that its image can be found in cave paintings from before the time of the Greeks and Romans. Yet it remains one of the favorite foods in our country today. You probably have some in your kitchen cabinet.

What is this wonder food? Tuna.

But its rich history is only half the story. Only recently have people come to appreciate the full value of this perfectly natural food. Tuna is high in protein, but low in calories and cholesterol, and has virtually no fat. In fact, tuna is lower in calories, cholesterol, and fat than most other meats, including beef, hamburger, pork, even chicken and many other fish. Tuna is so versatile too. Use it as a nutritious substitute for many meat and chicken dishes. And of course there's no beating that great StarKist taste.

Collected here for you is a variety of mouth-watering recipes that make it fun to enjoy tuna in more new and delicious ways than you ever imagined. They're all made with nutritious, easy-to-find ingredients, and they're all a snap to make—you can even use your microwave! Most of the recipes serve four, using the larger family sizes of StarKist and there's even an entire chapter of convenient recipes devoted solely to the single serving size can. No matter what size meal you're making, they're all guaranteed delicious.

So, when you're looking for a special dinner, try deliciously tangy, Sweet & Sour Tuna. Something fast and simple for the kids? How about Tuna 'n' Cheese Dogs. No matter what your pleasure, there is something here for everybody. So enjoy!

A Word About Timings and Calories

Preparation Time

Each recipe gives a preparation time that is based on the amount of time required to assemble the recipe before baking, cooking, chilling, freezing or serving. Times do not include chopping or cooking vegetables or cooking rice or pasta.

Microwave Cooking

Microwave cooking times in this publication are approximate. Numerous variables, such as the microwave oven's rated wattage and the starting temperature, shape, amount and depth of the foods, can affect cooking time. Use the cooking times as a guideline and check doneness before adding more time. Lower wattage ovens may consistently require longer cooking times.

Calorie Counts

A calorie count is given for each recipe. The calorie count is based on StarKist water-packed tuna. Recipes prepared with oil-packed tuna will be more. The calorie count does not include optional ingredients or serving suggestions. If more than one ingredient choice is listed, the first ingredient is used for the calorie count.

Classics
REVISITED

Wisconsin Tuna Cake with Lemon-Dill Sauce

For light frying, choose a nonstick skillet to make these tuna cakes.

1 can (12½ ounces) StarKist
    Tuna, drained and finely
    flaked
¾ cup seasoned bread crumbs
¼ cup minced green onions
2 tablespoons chopped drained
    pimiento

1 egg
½ cup low-fat milk
½ teaspoon grated lemon peel
2 tablespoons butter or
    margarine

Lemon-Dill Sauce

¼ cup chicken broth
1 tablespoon lemon juice

¼ teaspoon dill weed

• • •

Hot steamed shredded zucchini
    and carrots

Lemon slices

In a large bowl toss together tuna, bread crumbs, onions and pimiento. In a small bowl beat together egg and milk; stir in lemon peel. Stir into tuna mixture; toss until moistened. With lightly floured hands, shape mixture into eight 4-inch patties.

In a large nonstick skillet melt butter. Fry patties, a few at a time, until golden brown on both sides, about 3 minutes per side. Place on an ovenproof platter in a 300°F. oven until ready to serve.

For sauce, in a small saucepan heat broth, lemon juice and dill. For each serving, spoon shredded carrots and zucchini onto each plate; top with 2 tuna cakes. Top each cake with a half-slice lemon; spoon sauce over. Makes 4 servings.

Preparation time: 25 minutes
Calorie count: 278 calories, including 1 tablespoon sauce, per serving.

Wisconsin Tuna Cake with Lemon-Dill Sauce

Easy Niçoise Salad

Lettuce leaves
2 medium tomatoes, thinly sliced
1½ cups sliced cooked potatoes
1¼ cups cooked green beans
1 can (12½ ounces) StarKist
Tuna, drained and broken
into chunks

4 slices red or white onion,
separated into rings
½ cup sliced pitted ripe olives
1 hard-cooked egg, sliced
4 whole anchovies (optional)

Vinegar 'n' Oil Dressing

½ cup white vinegar
⅓ cup vegetable oil
1 tablespoon chopped parsley

½ teaspoon salt
¼ teaspoon pepper

On a large platter or 4 individual salad plates, arrange lettuce leaves. Arrange tomatoes, potatoes, beans, tuna, onion rings, olives and egg in a decorative design. Garnish with anchovies if desired.

For dressing, in a shaker jar combine remaining ingredients. Cover and shake until well blended. Drizzle some of the dressing over salad; serve remaining dressing. Makes 4 servings.

Preparation time: 20 minutes
Calorie count: 411 calories, including about ¼ cup dressing, per serving.

Veal Tonnato

Veal with tuna sauce is an old classic; you can serve this piquant cold sauce over almost any leftover meat.

1 can (3¼ ounces) StarKist Tuna,
drained and flaked
2 tablespoons olive oil
2 tablespoons dry white wine
1 tablespoon reduced-calorie
mayonnaise or salad dressing
1 clove garlic, minced

1 teaspoon dried basil, crushed
½ teaspoon dry mustard
¼ teaspoon white or black pepper
1 tablespoon chopped parsley
½ teaspoon drained capers
Sliced cold veal, roast beef or
turkey

In blender container or food processor bowl place tuna, oil, wine, mayonnaise, garlic, basil, mustard and pepper. Cover and process until nearly smooth. Stir in parsley and capers. Ladle about 3 tablespoons sauce over each serving of cold sliced meat. Makes 4 servings.

Preparation time: 10 minutes
Calorie count: 125 calories per serving of sauce.

Easy Niçoise Salad

Tuna Veronique

Besides toast, you can also serve this fruited tuna sauce over rice or pasta.

2 leeks or green onions
½ cup carrot cut into thin strips
1 stalk celery, cut diagonally into slices
1 tablespoon vegetable oil
1¾ cups or 1 can (14½ ounces) chicken broth
2 tablespoons cornstarch
⅓ cup dry white wine

1¼ cups seedless red and green grapes, cut into halves
1 can (12½ ounces) StarKist Tuna, drained and broken into chunks
1 tablespoon chopped chives
¼ teaspoon white or black pepper
4 to 5 slices bread, toasted and cut into quarters or 8 to 10 slices toasted French bread

If using leeks, wash thoroughly between leaves. Cut off white portion; trim and slice ¼ inch thick. Discard green portion. For green onions, trim and slice ¼ inch thick. In a large nonstick skillet sauté leeks, carrot and celery in oil for 3 minutes. In a small bowl stir together chicken broth and cornstarch until smooth; stir into vegetables. Cook and stir until mixture thickens and bubbles. Stir in wine; simmer for 2 minutes. Stir in grapes, tuna, chives and pepper. Cook for 2 minutes more to heat through. To serve, ladle sauce over toast points. Makes 4 to 5 servings.

Preparation time: 20 minutes
Calorie count: 273 calories per serving. (Based on 4 servings.)

Elaine's Tuna Tetrazzini

You can also use a combination of tuna and shrimp in this hearty pasta sauce.

8 ounces fresh mushrooms, sliced
1 cup chopped onion
2 tablespoons vegetable oil
3 tablespoons all-purpose flour
1 cup chicken broth
½ cup low-fat milk
½ teaspoon paprika
½ teaspoon salt
¼ teaspoon pepper

1 can (6½ ounces) StarKist Tuna, drained and broken into chunks
¼ cup grated Parmesan or Romano cheese
2 tablespoons minced parsley
8 ounces thin spaghetti or linguine, broken into halves, hot cooked

In a large skillet sauté mushrooms and onion in oil for 3 minutes, or until limp. Sprinkle flour over vegetables; stir until blended. Add chicken broth and milk all at once; cook and stir until mixture thickens and bubbles. Stir in paprika, salt and pepper; cook for 2 minutes more. Stir in tuna, cheese and parsley; cook for 1 to 2 minutes, or until heated through. Spoon over pasta. Makes 4 servings.

Preparation time: 20 minutes
Calorie count: 447 calories per serving.

Tuna Veronique

West Coast Bouillabaisse

This easy adaptation of the classic is faster and less expensive to make.

1 cup sliced onion
2 stalks celery, cut diagonally into slices
2 cloves garlic, minced
1 tablespoon vegetable oil
4 cups chicken broth
1 can (28 ounces) tomatoes with juice, cut up
1 can (6½ ounces) minced clams with juice
½ cup dry white wine
1 teaspoon Worcestershire sauce
½ teaspoon dried thyme, crushed
¼ teaspoon bottled hot pepper sauce
1 bay leaf
1 cup frozen cooked bay shrimp, thawed
1 can (6½ ounces) StarKist Tuna, drained and broken into chunks
Salt and pepper to taste
6 slices lemon
6 slices French bread

In a Dutch oven sauté onion, celery and garlic in oil for 3 minutes. Stir in broth, tomatoes with juice, clams with juice, wine, Worcestershire, thyme, hot pepper sauce and bay leaf. Bring to a boil; reduce heat. Simmer for 15 minutes. Stir in shrimp and tuna; cook for 2 minutes to heat. Remove bay leaf. Season with salt and pepper. Garnish with lemon slices and serve with bread. Makes 6 servings.

Preparation time: 15 minutes
Calorie count: 212 calories per serving with bread.

Tuna-Waldorf Salad Mold

Here's a cool summer salad to keep on hand for easy lunches and dinners.

1 package (6 ounces) lemon-flavored gelatin
2½ cups boiling water
1 cup apple juice
1 can (6½ ounces) StarKist Tuna, drained and flaked
1 cup finely chopped unpeeled apple
⅓ cup chopped pecans or walnuts
⅓ cup finely chopped celery
⅓ cup reduced-calorie mayonnaise or salad dressing
3 tablespoons low-fat milk

In a large, shallow bowl dissolve gelatin in boiling water. Stir in apple juice until blended. Cover; chill mixture about 30 minutes, or until the consistency of unbeaten egg whites. Fold in tuna, apple, pecans and celery. Spray a 4- or 5-cup mold (or 5 individual 1-cup molds) with aerosol shortening; pour in mixture. Cover; chill several hours until set. For dressing, in a small bowl stir together mayonnaise and milk; serve with salad. Makes 4 main-dish or 8 side-dish servings.

Preparation time: 15 minutes
Calorie count: 374 calories, including about 2 tablespoons dressing, per main-dish serving; 187 calories, including about 1 tablespoon dressing, per side-dish serving.

West Coast Bouillabaisse

Tuna Loaf

This meat loaf tastes like a turkey or chicken loaf topped with cheese. Serve any leftover loaf sliced cold for next day's sandwiches.

1 cup grated peeled potato
1 cup grated carrots
1 can (12½ ounces) StarKist Tuna, drained and finely flaked
½ cup chopped green onions
⅓ cup chopped parsley
1 tablespoon chopped drained pimiento

1 clove garlic, minced
2 eggs
1 teaspoon dried thyme, crushed
¼ teaspoon ground sage
½ teaspoon salt
¼ teaspoon pepper
2 tablespoons cornstarch
⅔ cup shredded low-fat mozzarella or Cheddar cheese

Preheat oven to 350°F. Spray an 8×4×2½-inch loaf pan with aerosol shortening. In a saucepan steam potato and carrots over simmering water for 5 minutes, or until tender. In a large bowl stir together tuna, potato, carrots, onions, parsley, pimiento and garlic until well combined. In a small bowl stir together eggs and seasonings; stir in cornstarch. Mix into tuna mixture. Transfer mixture to loaf pan. Cover with foil. Bake for 20 minutes. Uncover; bake for 10 minutes more, or until heated through. Sprinkle cheese over top; bake for 1 to 2 minutes, or until cheese is melted. Let stand for 5 minutes; slice. Makes 4 to 6 servings.

Preparation time: 25 minutes
Calorie count: 293 calories per serving. (Based on 4 servings.)

Baked Tuna Croquettes with Dill Sauce

The piquant Dill Sauce really enhances these crisp croquettes.

2 tablespoons butter or margarine
1 tablespoon all-purpose flour
½ cup low-fat milk
1 can (12½ ounces) StarKist Tuna, drained and finely flaked
1 cup grated zucchini or yellow squash

2 tablespoons minced green onion
1 tablespoon lemon juice
1 teaspoon dried thyme, crushed
¼ teaspoon pepper
½ cup buttermilk or low-fat milk
1 egg
1½ cups crushed cornflakes
⅓ cup grated Parmesan or Romano cheese

Dill Sauce

1 cup plain low-fat yogurt
⅓ cup finely minced cucumber

½ teaspoon dill weed

Preheat oven to 350°F. In a medium saucepan melt butter; stir in flour. Add milk all at once. Cook and stir until mixture thickens and bubbles. Cook for 2 minutes more. Remove from heat. Stir in tuna, zucchini, onion, lemon juice, thyme and pepper until well combined. Cover and chill mixture for 30 minutes. Shape chilled mixture into eight 2-inch balls. In a shallow dish stir together buttermilk and egg. In another shallow dish combine cornflakes and cheese. Roll balls first in egg mixture, then in cornflake mixture. Repeat procedure to coat well. Spray a baking sheet with aerosol shortening; arrange croquettes on baking sheet. Bake, uncovered, about 30 minutes, or until heated through. For Dill Sauce, in a small bowl stir together yogurt, cucumber and dill. Serve sauce with croquettes. Makes 4 servings; 2 croquettes per serving.

Preparation time: 15 minutes
Calorie count: 342 calories, including ⅓ cup sauce, per serving.

Tuna Lasagne

1 cup diced zucchini
1 cup sliced fresh mushrooms
½ cup sliced green onions
1 clove garlic, minced
2 tablespoons vegetable oil
1 can (12½ ounces) StarKist Tuna, drained and broken into chunks
1½ cups spaghetti sauce
½ teaspoon dried thyme or basil, crushed
½ teaspoon dried oregano, crushed
1½ cups low-fat cottage cheese
1 extra-large egg
6 lasagne noodles, cooked and drained
3 slices low-fat mozzarella cheese, cut into ½-inch strips
2 tablespoons grated Parmesan or Romano cheese
2 tablespoons chopped parsley

In a large skillet sauté zucchini, mushrooms, onions and garlic in oil for 3 minutes, or until vegetables are nearly tender. Stir in tuna, spaghetti sauce and herbs; bring to a boil. Remove from heat.

Preheat oven to 375°F. In a small bowl stir together cottage cheese and egg. Spray an 11×7×2-inch baking dish with aerosol shortening. Spread ½ cup of the tuna mixture on bottom of dish. Place 3 lasagne noodles over sauce; layer ½ of the cottage cheese mixture, then ½ of the remaining tuna mixture, spreading evenly. Place ½ of the mozzarella cheese strips over tuna layer. Repeat layers, ending with mozzarella. Sprinkle Parmesan over top. Cover with foil; bake for 30 minutes. Uncover; bake for 10 minutes more, or until sauce is bubbly and lasagne is heated through. Let stand for 5 minutes. Sprinkle with parsley; cut into squares to serve. Makes 4 to 6 servings.

Preparation time: 40 minutes
Calorie count: 437 calories per serving. (Based on 4 servings.)

Tuna-Stuffed Bell Peppers

4 large red, green or yellow bell peppers
½ cup vegetables*
¼ cup chopped green onions
1 clove garlic, minced
2 tablespoons vegetable oil
1 cup cooked pasta or rice
1 can (12½ ounces) StarKist Tuna, drained and flaked
1 medium tomato, chopped
⅓ cup niblet corn
1 egg, beaten
½ teaspoon dried thyme, crushed
Salt and pepper to taste
½ cup shredded low-fat mozzarella cheese
Chopped parsley

Cut peppers lengthwise into halves. Remove seeds and ribs from peppers. Place peppers in boiling water for 3 minutes. Rinse; drain, cut side down. Set aside.

Preheat oven to 375°F. For stuffing, in a medium skillet sauté vegetables with onions and garlic in oil for 3 minutes. Stir in pasta, tuna, tomato, corn, egg and seasonings. Cook until heated through. Spray a shallow baking dish with aerosol shortening. Place shells, cut side up, in dish. Spoon tuna mixture into shells, mounding if necessary. Bake for 15 minutes. Sprinkle with cheese and parsley. Bake for 5 minutes, or until cheese is melted. Makes 4 servings.

*Suggested vegetables are: green peas, French-cut green beans, chopped zucchini or broccoli florets.

Preparation time: 30 minutes
Calorie count: 344 calories per serving.

Tomatoes Stuffed with Hot Tuna Salad

Try this recipe when summer tomatoes are at their peak of flavor.

4 large tomatoes
1 can (9¼ ounces) StarKist Tuna, drained and flaked
1 cup cubed Swiss or Cheddar cheese (¼-inch cubes)
1 cup cooked macaroni
¼ cup minced onion
¼ cup reduced-calorie mayonnaise or salad dressing
¼ cup reduced-calorie sour cream
Chopped parsley

Preheat oven to 350°F. Cut a slice from tops of tomatoes. Hollow out tomato. Spray a casserole with aerosol shortening; place tomatoes in dish.

In a bowl combine tuna, cheese, macaroni and onion. Stir in mayonnaise and sour cream. Spoon into shells. Replace tops. Cover and bake for 30 to 40 minutes, or until heated. Sprinkle with parsley. Makes 4 servings.

Preparation time: 20 minutes
Calorie count: 445 calories per serving.

Tuna-Stuffed Bell Peppers

No Fuss Tuna Quiche

Frozen or refrigerated rolled pastry works well for this recipe.

1 unbaked 9-inch deep dish
pastry shell
1½ cups low-fat milk
3 extra-large eggs
⅓ cup chopped green onions
1 tablespoon chopped drained
pimiento

1 teaspoon dried basil, crushed
½ teaspoon salt
1 can (6½ ounces) StarKist Tuna,
drained and flaked
½ cup shredded low-fat Cheddar
cheese
8 spears (4 inches each) broccoli

Preheat oven to 450°F. Bake pastry shell for 5 minutes; remove to rack to cool. Reduce oven temperature to 325°F.

For filling, in a bowl whisk together milk and eggs. Stir in onions, pimiento, basil and salt. Fold in tuna and cheese. Pour into prebaked pastry shell. Bake at 325°F. for 30 minutes. Meanwhile, in a saucepan steam broccoli spears over simmering water for 5 minutes. Drain; set aside. After 30 minutes, arrange broccoli spears, spoke-fashion, over quiche. Bake for 25 to 35 minutes, or until a knife inserted 2 inches from center comes out clean. Let stand for 5 minutes. Cut into 8 wedges, centering a broccoli spear in each wedge. Makes 8 servings.

Note: If desired, 1 cup chopped broccoli may be added to the filling before baking.

Preparation time: 20 minutes
Calorie count: 226 calories per serving.

Tuna & Mushroom Stroganoff

3 cups sliced fresh mushrooms
½ cup chopped green onions
2 cloves garlic, minced
2 tablespoons vegetable oil
2 tablespoons all-purpose flour
1½ cups low-fat milk
½ teaspoon dried tarragon,
crushed

½ teaspoon Worcestershire sauce
¼ teaspoon pepper
1 can (12½ ounces) StarKist
Tuna, drained and broken
into chunks
⅓ cup reduced-calorie sour cream
⅓ cup plain low-fat yogurt
Hot cooked pasta or rice

In a large skillet sauté mushrooms, onions and garlic in oil for 3 minutes, stirring frequently. Sprinkle flour over vegetables; stir until blended. Add milk all at once; cook and stir until mixture thickens and bubbles. Stir in tarragon, Worcestershire and pepper. Add tuna, sour cream and yogurt. Cook over low heat for 2 minutes, or until heated. (Do not boil.) Serve over pasta. Makes 4 to 6 servings.

Preparation time: 20 minutes
Calorie count: 400 calories, including 1 cup cooked pasta, per serving. (Based on 4 servings.)

Single SERVING

Puffy Tuna Omelet

A puffy omelet is simple to make and it's a bit more special for a single serving.

2 eggs, separated
¼ teaspoon pepper
1 tablespoon water
1 tablespoon butter or margarine
2 tablespoons chicken broth
½ small red or green bell pepper,
    cut into strips
1 cup chopped spinach leaves

1 can (3¼ ounces) StarKist Tuna,
    drained and broken into
    chunks
¼ teaspoon dried oregano,
    crushed
  Salt and pepper to taste
2 teaspoons grated Parmesan
    cheese

In a small bowl beat egg yolks and pepper on high speed of electric mixer about 5 minutes, or until thick and lemon-colored. In a medium bowl beat egg whites and water until stiff peaks form. Pour yolks over whites and gently fold in.

Preheat oven to 325°F. In a 7-inch nonstick skillet with ovenproof handle melt butter over low heat. Lift and tilt skillet to coat sides. Pour egg mixture into hot skillet, mounding it slightly higher around edges. Cook over low heat about 6 minutes, or until eggs are puffed and set and bottom is golden brown. Bake for 6 to 8 minutes, or until a knife inserted near center comes out clean.

Meanwhile, in a small skillet heat chicken broth. Cook and stir bell pepper and spinach in broth for 2 minutes. Stir in tuna and oregano; season to taste with salt and pepper. Drain; keep warm. Loosen sides of omelet with spatula. Make a shallow cut across omelet, cutting slightly off center; fill with tuna mixture. Fold smaller portion of omelet over larger portion. Sprinkle with cheese. Serve immediately. Makes 1 serving.

Preparation time: 10 minutes
Calorie count: 422 calories per serving.

Puffy Tuna Omelet

Tuna-Lettuce Bundles

This salad makes one hearty serving; smaller appetites may want to save a portion of this salad for the next day's lunch.

2 large leaves leaf lettuce
1 can (3¼ ounces) StarKist Tuna,
    drained and broken into
    small chunks
½ cup shredded red cabbage
¼ cup shredded zucchini

¼ cup alfalfa sprouts
1 tablespoon reduced-calorie
    Thousand Island or blue
    cheese dressing
Pepper to taste
2 red or green bell pepper rings

Trim stalks from lettuce leaves. In a small bowl toss together tuna, cabbage, zucchini and sprouts. Stir in dressing; season to taste with pepper. Spoon ½ of the salad mixture in center of each leaf. Roll up leaves, enclosing filling. Secure lettuce bundles by slipping a bell pepper ring over each. Place bundles seam side down on plate. Makes 1 serving.

Preparation time: 10 minutes
Calorie count: 190 calories per serving.

Tuna-Citrus Salad with Honey Dressing

1 orange, tangerine or ½ large
    pink grapefruit, peeled,
    seeded and sectioned
1 can (3¼ ounces) StarKist Tuna,
    drained and broken into
    chunks

¼ cup sliced fresh mushrooms
Lettuce leaves
2 tablespoons chopped green
    onion

Honey Dressing

2 tablespoons vegetable oil
2 tablespoons white wine vinegar

1 to 2 teaspoons honey
⅛ teaspoon pepper

Arrange citrus, tuna and mushrooms on lettuce-lined plate. Sprinkle with onion. In a shaker jar combine remaining ingredients. Cover and shake until well blended. Pour over salad. Makes 1 serving.

Preparation time: 15 minutes
Calorie count: 484 calories per serving.

Fettucine à la Tuna

½ cup broccoli florets
½ cup chopped red bell pepper
1 tablespoon sliced green onion
1 clove garlic, minced
1 tablespoon butter or margarine
¼ cup low-fat milk
¼ cup low-fat ricotta cheese
   Salt and pepper to taste

1 can (3¼ ounces) StarKist Tuna,
   drained and broken into
   small chunks
2 ounces fettucine or linguine,
   cooked and drained
1 tablespoon grated Parmesan or
   Romano cheese (optional)

In a saucepan steam broccoli and bell pepper over simmering water for 5 minutes. Drain liquid from vegetables and remove steamer. In same pan sauté onion and garlic in butter for 2 minutes. Add milk and ricotta cheese, stirring well with wire whisk. Season to taste with salt and pepper. Add tuna and vegetables; cook over low heat for 2 minutes more. Toss fettucine with tuna mixture. Spoon onto plate; sprinkle with Parmesan cheese if desired. Makes 1 serving.

Preparation time: 15 minutes
Calorie count: 415 calories per serving.

Gazpacho Tuna Salad

*If you like gazpacho, that tomato-based soup filled with crisp, cold vegetables,
you'll enjoy this salad takeoff.*

1 cup shredded lettuce
1 can (3¼ ounces) StarKist Tuna,
   drained and flaked
⅓ cup chopped carrot
⅓ cup chopped celery
⅓ cup chopped cucumber or
   zucchini

⅓ cup tomato-vegetable juice
1 tablespoon vegetable oil
   Bottled hot pepper sauce to
   taste
2 tablespoons croutons

Line a dinner plate with shredded lettuce. In a large shaker jar combine tuna, chopped vegetables, vegetable juice, oil and hot pepper sauce to taste. Cover and shake until well blended. Use a slotted spoon to arrange mixture over lettuce-lined plate; sprinkle croutons over salad. Makes 1 serving.

Preparation time: 15 minutes
Calorie count: 371 calories per serving.

Individual Pizza

Flour tortillas make handy, low-calorie pizza "crusts" for individual pizzas.

1 (8-inch) flour tortilla
¼ cup spaghetti sauce or pizza
   sauce
1 can (3¼ ounces) StarKist Tuna,
   drained and broken into
   small chunks

¼ cup sliced mushrooms
¼ cup tomato slices
2 green or red bell pepper rings,
   cut into halves
¼ cup shredded low-fat Cheddar
   or mozzarella cheese

Preheat oven to 375°F. Place tortilla on a small baking sheet. Bake for 5 minutes, or until tortilla begins to crisp. Spread spaghetti sauce to within ½ inch of edge. Sprinkle tuna, mushrooms and tomato over tortilla. Arrange bell pepper half-rings on top. Sprinkle cheese over pizza. Bake for 8 to 10 minutes more, or until heated through. Makes 1 serving.

Preparation time: 10 minutes
Calorie count: 366 calories per serving.

Tuna Poor-Boy

If you've never thought about making a submarine sandwich with tuna, this easy interpretation is worth sampling.

1 individual French or poor-boy
   sandwich roll, split
1 can (3¼ ounces) StarKist Tuna,
   drained and flaked
2 tablespoons reduced-calorie
   mayonnaise or salad dressing
1 tablespoon chopped pickle
   relish
   Lettuce leaves

1 slice red onion, separated into
   rings
2 rings red or green bell pepper
2 large slices tomato
1 slice (1 ounce) reduced-calorie
   American cheese, cut
   diagonally into halves
   Pickled chili peppers (optional)

Toast roll if desired. In a small bowl stir together tuna, mayonnaise and pickle relish. Arrange lettuce over bottom half of roll; spoon tuna mixture over lettuce. Top with onion rings, bell pepper rings, tomato slices and cheese. Replace top half of roll; cut sandwich in half crosswise. Serve with pickled chili peppers if desired. Makes 1 large sandwich.

Preparation time: 15 minutes
Calorie count: 475 calories per serving.

Tuna-Papaya-Avocado Salad

You can substitute ripe pears, peaches or plums for the papaya.

1 can (3¼ ounces) StarKist Tuna, drained and broken into chunks
Lettuce leaves

½ ripe papaya, peeled, seeded and thinly sliced
¼ medium-ripe avocado, peeled, pitted and thinly sliced

Dressing

2 tablespoons orange juice
1 tablespoon vegetable or olive oil

1 teaspoon honey
Dash pepper

• • •

Strawberry or orange wedges for garnish (optional)

Mound tuna in center of lettuce-lined plate. Surround with slices of papaya and avocado. For dressing, in a small shaker jar combine orange juice, oil, honey and pepper. Cover and shake until well blended. Drizzle over salad. Garnish with strawberry if desired. Makes 1 serving.

Preparation time: 10 minutes
Calorie count: 400 calories per serving.

Tuna Cobb Salad

Using tuna in this classic salad keeps the calorie count manageable.

1 cup chopped lettuce
½ medium-ripe avocado, peeled, seeded and diced
½ medium tomato, chopped
1 can (3¼ ounces) StarKist Tuna, drained and broken into chunks

2 slices bacon, cooked and crumbled
1 hard-cooked egg, chopped
¼ cup reduced-calorie blue cheese salad dressing
Pepper to taste

In a medium bowl toss together lettuce and all ingredients except salad dressing and pepper. Add dressing; toss until coated. Sprinkle with pepper; transfer to dinner plate. Makes 1 serving.

Preparation time: 15 minutes
Calorie count: 491 calories per serving.

Tuna-Papaya-Avocado Salad

Tuna Ramen Noodle Salad

½ package (3 ounces) Oriental-flavor ramen noodle soup mix

1 can (3¼ ounces) StarKist Tuna, drained and flaked

½ cup julienne-strip cucumber

½ cup julienne-strip green or red bell pepper

½ cup sliced water chestnuts, cut into halves

Almond Dressing

2 tablespoons rice or white vinegar

2 teaspoons sesame oil

1 teaspoon peanut butter

⅛ teaspoon crushed red pepper

Cook ramen noodles according to package directions. Drain broth, reserving if desired to use as a clear soup for another meal. In a medium bowl toss noodles with tuna, cucumber, bell pepper and water chestnuts.

For Almond Dressing, in a small shaker jar combine vinegar, oil, peanut butter and crushed red pepper. Cover and shake until well blended. Toss with noodle mixture. Serve immediately. Makes 1 serving.

Preparation time: 15 minutes
Calorie count: 416 calories per serving.

Tuna Chowder for One

If you like, vary the vegetables by using mixed vegetable combinations packaged for single servings.

2 tablespoons chopped green onion

½ cup diced mixed vegetables

1 tablespoon vegetable oil

1 tablespoon all-purpose flour

1¼ cups low-fat milk

½ teaspoon fines herbes or dried basil, crushed

⅛ teaspoon paprika

1 can (3¼ ounces) StarKist Tuna, drained and flaked

Salt and pepper to taste

In a 2-quart saucepan sauté onion and mixed vegetables in oil about 3 minutes, or until vegetables are crisp-tender. Stir in flour until blended. Add milk all at once. Add fines herbes and paprika; cook and stir until mixture thickens and bubbles. Reduce heat; stir in tuna. Cook for 2 minutes more to heat through. Season to taste with salt and pepper. Makes 1 serving.

Preparation time: 15 minutes
Calorie count: 438 calories per serving.

Tuna Ramen Noodle Salad

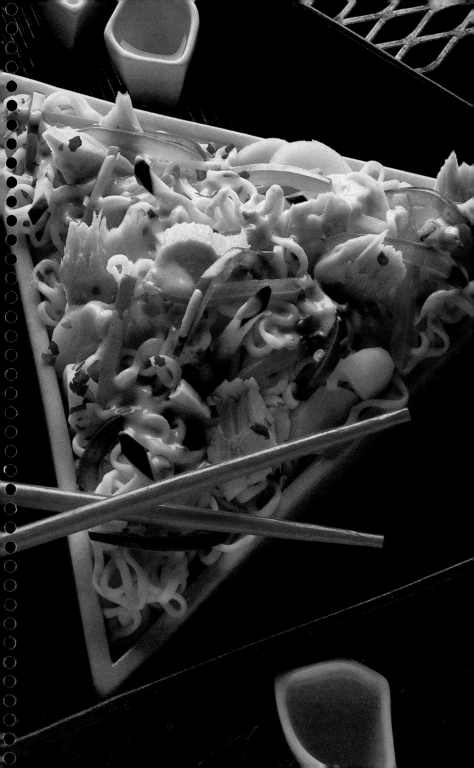

Light 'n' Easy
SUPPERS

Tuna & Vegetables à la Grecque

This makes a terrific cold salad for any meal, and it's superb for picnics.

1½ cups French-cut green beans, cooked
1 cup cherry tomatoes, cut into halves or tomato wedges
1 cup sliced cooked carrots
1 cup sliced yellow squash or zucchini

½ cup slivered green bell pepper
1 can (12½ ounces) StarKist Tuna, drained and broken into chunks

Red Vinaigrette

⅓ cup red wine vinegar
¼ cup olive or vegetable oil
2 tablespoons chopped parsley
1 teaspoon sugar

1 teaspoon dried rosemary, crushed
1 clove garlic, crushed
Salt and pepper to taste

In a large nonmetallic bowl stir together beans, tomatoes, carrots, squash, bell pepper and tuna. For Red Vinaigrette dressing, in a large shaker jar combine remaining ingredients. Cover and shake until well blended. Pour over salad. Toss salad to coat. Cover and chill 2 to 24 hours before serving. Serve salad with a slotted spoon. Makes 4 to 5 servings.

Preparation time: 15 minutes
Calorie count: 273 calories per serving. (Based on 4 servings.)

Tuna & Vegetables à la Grecque

Tuna & Fresh Fruit Salad

Use in-season fruits to enjoy this salad at any time of year.

Lettuce leaves (optional)
1 can (12½ ounces) StarKist
Tuna, drained and broken
into chunks

4 cups slices or wedges fresh
fruit*
¼ cup slivered almonds (optional)

Fruit Dressing

1 container (8 ounces) lemon,
mandarin orange or vanilla
low-fat yogurt

2 tablespoons orange juice
¼ teaspoon ground cinnamon

Line a large platter or 4 individual plates with lettuce leaves if desired. Arrange tuna and desired fruit in a decorative design over lettuce. Sprinkle almonds over salad if desired.

For Fruit Dressing, in a small bowl stir together yogurt, orange juice and cinnamon until well blended. Serve dressing with salad. Makes 4 servings.

*Suggested fruits are: pineapple, melon, apples, pears, peaches, kiwifruit, bananas, berries, papaya or citrus fruit.

Preparation time: 15 minutes
Calorie count: 233 calories, including about ¼ cup dressing, per serving.

Tuna-Vegetable Chowder

1½ cups chopped vegetables*
2 tablespoons butter or
margarine
¼ cup all-purpose flour
2⅔ cups low-fat milk or buttermilk
1 cup chicken broth

1 can (6½ ounces) StarKist Tuna,
drained and flaked
1½ teaspoons dried chervil, basil or
Italian seasoning, crushed
¼ teaspoon pepper
2 tablespoons sherry (optional)

In a saucepan steam vegetables over simmering water for 5 to 8 minutes, or until almost tender. Set aside.

In a large saucepan melt butter; stir in flour. Add milk and broth all at once. Cook and stir until mixture thickens and bubbles. Cook and stir for 2 minutes more. Stir in cooked vegetables, tuna, herb and pepper. Cook for 2 minutes to heat through. Stir in sherry. Makes 4 to 5 servings.

*Suggested vegetables are: broccoli, cauliflower, carrot, zucchini, mushrooms or a combination.

Preparation time: 15 minutes
Calorie count: 245 calories per serving. (Based on 4 servings.)

Tuna & Fresh Fruit Salad

Tuna in Red Pepper Sauce

Pureed red bell peppers are the base for a rich red wine sauce.

2 cups chopped red bell peppers (about 2 peppers)
½ cup chopped onion
1 clove garlic, minced
2 tablespoons vegetable oil

¼ cup dry red or white wine
¼ cup chicken broth
2 teaspoons sugar
¼ teaspoon pepper

• • •

1 red bell pepper, slivered and cut into ½-inch pieces
1 yellow or green bell pepper, slivered and cut into ½-inch pieces

½ cup julienne-strip carrots
1 can (9¼ ounces) StarKist Tuna, drained and broken into chunks
Hot cooked pasta or rice

In a skillet sauté the chopped bell pepper, onion and garlic in oil for 5 minutes, or until vegetables are very tender. In a blender container or food processor bowl place vegetable mixture; cover and process until pureed. Return to pan; stir in wine, chicken broth, sugar and pepper. Keep warm. In a 2-quart saucepan steam bell pepper pieces and carrots over simmering water for 5 minutes. Stir steamed vegetables into sauce with tuna; cook for 2 minutes, or until heated through. Serve tuna mixture over pasta. Makes 4 to 5 servings.

Preparation time: 20 minutes
Calorie count: 284 calories, including 2 ounces cooked pasta, per serving. (Based on 4 servings.)

Tuna Frittata

"Frittata" is simply a fancy name for an open-faced omelet.

1 cup thinly sliced zucchini
½ cup thinly sliced onion
2 tablespoons vegetable oil
5 extra-large eggs
¼ cup low-fat milk

1 can (3¼ ounces) StarKist Tuna, drained and flaked
½ teaspoon salt
¼ teaspoon pepper
½ cup shredded Swiss or Monterey Jack cheese

In a large ovenproof skillet sauté zucchini and onion in oil for 3 minutes, or until vegetables are limp. In a medium bowl beat eggs lightly with milk. Stir in tuna, salt and pepper. Preheat broiler. Pour egg mixture over sautéed vegetables; reduce heat to medium. Cook, covered, for 5 to 8 minutes, or until set. Uncover frittata; sprinkle cheese over top. Place frittata under broiler until cheese is melted. Cut into quarters to serve. Makes 4 servings.

Preparation time: 15 minutes
Calorie count: 282 calories per serving.

Tuna in Red Pepper Sauce

"Grilled" Tuna with Vegetables in Herb Butter

Serve with a fruit salad and warm bread.

4 pieces heavy-duty aluminum
  foil, each 12×18 inches
1 can (12½ ounces) StarKist
  Tuna, drained and broken
  into chunks
1 cup slivered red or green bell
  pepper
1 cup slivered yellow squash or
  zucchini
1 cup pea pods, cut crosswise into
  halves

1 cup slivered carrots
4 green onions, cut into 2-inch
  slices
¼ cup butter or margarine, melted
1 tablespoon lemon or lime juice
1 clove garlic, minced
2 teaspoons dried tarragon,
  crushed
1 teaspoon dill weed
  Salt and pepper to taste

On each piece of foil mound tuna, bell pepper, squash, pea pods, carrots and
onions. For herb butter, in a small bowl stir together butter, lemon juice, garlic,
tarragon and dill weed. Drizzle over tuna and vegetables. Sprinkle with salt and
pepper. Fold edges of each foil square together to make packets.

To grill: Place foil packets about 4 inches above hot coals. Grill for 10 to 12
minutes, or until heated through, turning packet over halfway through grill time.

To bake: Place foil packets on a baking sheet. Bake in preheated 450°F. oven for
15 to 20 minutes, or until heated through.

To serve, cut an "X" on top of each packet; peel back the foil. Makes 4 servings.

Preparation time: 25 minutes
Calorie count: 235 calories per serving.

Scrambled Eggs with Tuna & Onions

6 extra-large eggs
½ cup low-fat milk
1 can (3¼ ounces) StarKist Tuna,
  drained and flaked
1 tablespoon chopped green
  chilies (optional)

¼ teaspoon bottled hot pepper
  sauce
½ cup chopped green onions
1 tablespoon butter or margarine

In a bowl whisk together eggs and milk. Add tuna, chilies and hot pepper sauce;
stir. In a nonstick skillet sauté onions in butter for 2 minutes. Add egg mixture.
Cook, stirring frequently, over medium heat until mixture begins to set. Continue
lifting and folding partially cooked eggs to allow uncooked portion to flow
underneath. Cook until eggs are cooked but still moist. Makes 4 servings.

Preparation time: 10 minutes
Calorie count: 212 calories per serving.

"Grilled" Tuna with Vegetables in Herb Butter

Tuna in Squash Shells

Yellow crookneck squash or yellow zucchini make pretty containers for the filling.

4 medium zucchini, yellow
    zucchini or yellow crookneck
    squash
¼ cup diced carrot
¼ cup chopped green onions
2 tablespoons bottled reduced-
    calorie Italian dressing

1 can (9¼ ounces) StarKist Tuna,
    drained and flaked
¼ cup cooked white or brown rice
¼ teaspoon garlic powder
¼ teaspoon pepper
½ cup shredded low-fat Cheddar,
    Swiss or mozzarella cheese

Cut squash lengthwise into halves. Trim a very thin slice from bottom of each squash half so it will sit upright. Scoop out the pulp from each squash half, leaving ¼-inch-thick shells. Chop the pulp. Place squash shells in boiling water to cover for 5 minutes. Rinse in cold water. Drain shells well, upside down, on paper towels. Set aside.

Preheat oven to 375°F. For filling, in a skillet sauté carrot, onions and chopped squash pulp in Italian dressing for 3 minutes. Stir in tuna, rice and seasonings until well combined. Mound filling mixture in shells. Spray a shallow baking dish with aerosol shortening. Place shells in dish; cover with foil. Bake for 20 minutes. Uncover; top with cheese. Bake for 5 minutes more, or until heated through. Makes 4 servings; 2 shells per serving.

Preparation time: 25 minutes
Calorie count: 192 calories per serving.

Tuna & Ham Risotto

1 cup diced cooked ham
1 cup shredded carrots
2 leeks, white part only, sliced or
    ⅔ cup sliced onion
1 stalk celery, cut diagonally into
    thin slices
2 tablespoons olive or vegetable
    oil
2 cups beef or chicken broth

½ cup dry white wine
¾ cup long-grain rice
1 teaspoon dried Italian
    seasoning, crushed
1 can (9¼ ounces) StarKist Tuna,
    drained and broken into
    chunks
2 tablespoons chopped parsley
2 tablespoons tomato paste

In a deep skillet or 3-quart saucepan sauté ham, carrots, leeks and celery in oil for 3 to 5 minutes, or until vegetables are tender. Stir in broth and wine; bring mixture to a boil. Stir in rice and Italian seasoning; reduce heat to medium-low. Simmer, covered, about 20 minutes, or until most of the liquid is absorbed. Stir in tuna, parsley and tomato paste; heat through. Makes 4 servings.

Preparation time: 20 minutes
Calorie count: 293 calories per serving.

Tuna in Squash Shells

Tuna Tacos

The garbanzo beans are a calorie-smart substitute for refried beans, since they do not contain any of the animal fat often used in refried beans.

1 can (6½ ounces) StarKist Tuna, drained and flaked
⅓ cup chopped green onions
¼ cup bottled salsa
2 cups shredded lettuce
8 corn taco shells*
1 cup garbanzo beans
1 cup chopped tomato
⅓ cup sliced pitted ripe olives
Salsa, shredded low-fat cheese, diced avocado, chopped green chilies for toppings (optional)

In a medium bowl toss together tuna, onions and salsa until combined. To assemble tacos, sprinkle lettuce into each taco shell. Divide tuna mixture among tacos, along with garbanzo beans, tomato and olives. Garnish as desired with toppings. Makes 4 servings; 2 tacos per serving.

*Substitute 8 (6-inch) flour tortillas for the taco shells if soft tacos are preferred.

Preparation time: 20 minutes
Calorie count: 273 calories per serving. Toppings are extra.

Tuna Thermador

Serve this sophisticated adaptation of lobster thermador in individual casseroles or as a sauce over pasta, rice or spaghetti squash.

2 shallots, peeled and sliced or ¼ cup chopped green onions
1 tablespoon vegetable oil
2 tablespoons all-purpose flour
1 cup low-fat milk
1 can (12½ ounces) StarKist Tuna, drained and broken into chunks
1½ cups julienne-strip carrots, steamed
¼ cup dry white wine
1 teaspoon dried chervil
1 teaspoon dried tarragon, crushed
½ teaspoon dry mustard
1 tablespoon grated Parmesan or Romano cheese
1 tablespoon chopped parsley

In a saucepan sauté shallots in oil for 2 minutes. Stir in flour. Add milk all at once. Cook and stir until mixture thickens and bubbles; cook for 2 minutes. Remove from heat; stir in tuna, carrots, wine, chervil, tarragon and mustard.

Preheat oven to 350°F. Divide mixture among 4 individual ramekins or spoon into a 9×9×2-inch shallow casserole. Sprinkle with cheese and parsley. Cover with foil. Bake for 25 to 30 minutes, or until heated through. Makes 4 servings.

Preparation time: 15 minutes
Calorie count: 214 calories per serving.

Tuna Tacos

Entertaining IDEAS

Tuna-Stuffed Artichokes

Fresh artichokes should have tightly closed leaves and a compact shape.

4 medium artichokes
  Lemon juice
1½ cups chopped fresh mushrooms
1 cup diced yellow squash or
  zucchini
⅓ cup chopped green onions
1 clove garlic, minced
2 tablespoons vegetable oil

1 can (12½ ounces) StarKist
  Tuna, drained and flaked
½ cup shredded low-fat Cheddar,
  mozzarella or Monterey Jack
  cheese
¼ cup seasoned bread crumbs
2 tablespoons diced drained
  pimiento

With a kitchen shear trim sharp points from artichoke leaves. Trim stems; remove loose outer leaves. Cut 1 inch from the tops. Brush cut edges with lemon juice. In a large covered saucepan or Dutch oven bring artichokes and salted water to a boil; reduce heat. Simmer until a leaf pulls out easily, 20 to 30 minutes. Drain upside down.

Preheat oven to 450°F. When cool enough to handle, cut artichokes lengthwise into halves. Remove fuzzy chokes and hearts. Finely chop hearts; discard chokes. In a medium skillet sauté mushrooms, artichoke hearts, squash, onions and garlic in oil for 3 minutes, stirring frequently. Stir in tuna. Place artichoke halves, cut side up, in a lightly oiled baking dish. Mound tuna mixture in center of artichokes. In a small bowl stir together cheese, bread crumbs and pimiento; sprinkle over filling. Bake for 5 to 8 minutes, or until cheese is melted and topping is golden. Makes 4 main-dish or 8 appetizer servings.

Preparation time: 35 minutes
Calorie count: 272 calories per main-dish serving; 136 calories per appetizer serving.

Tuna-Stuffed Artichokes

Tuna Antipasto

Serve this as a main-course salad or a first-course appetizer.

1 can (12½ ounces) StarKist
  Tuna, drained and broken
  into chunks
1 jar (14 ounces) marinated
  artichoke hearts
1 jar (4 ounces) small whole
  mushrooms, drained
  Lettuce leaves
1 can (8 ounces) garbanzo beans,
  drained and rinsed

1 jar (7 ounces) roasted peppers,
  well drained and cut into
  quarters
1 can (6 ounces) pitted ripe or
  stuffed green olives, drained
½ small red onion, thinly sliced
1 large tomato, sliced
6 to 8 thin slices low-fat
  mozzarella, Fontina or
  Monterey Jack cheese
  French or Italian bread slices

In a medium, nonmetal bowl place tuna, artichoke hearts with marinade and mushrooms. Toss gently; cover and chill 4 to 24 hours. Remove tuna, artichokes and mushrooms with a slotted spoon and mound in center of a lettuce-lined platter. Arrange garbanzos, roasted peppers, olives, onion, tomato and cheese around tuna mixture. Serve with French bread slices. Makes 4 to 6 main-dish or 8 appetizer servings.

Preparation time: 20 minutes
Calorie count: 488 calories per main-dish serving; 244 calories per appetizer serving. Bread is extra. (Based on 4 main-dish servings.)

Tuna Mousse with Parsley Sauce

Use any decorative mold or bowl to shape this easy mousse, which makes a perfect light appetizer or first course.

1 envelope unflavored gelatin
¼ cup cold water
½ cup boiling chicken broth
½ cup reduced-calorie mayonnaise
  or salad dressing
1 tablespoon lemon or lime juice

1 can (12½ ounces) StarKist
  Tuna, drained and flaked
½ cup shredded peeled cucumber
½ cup shredded carrot
2 egg whites, beaten until stiff

Parsley Sauce

½ cup plain low-fat yogurt
½ cup reduced-calorie cream
  cheese
1 cup parsley sprigs

1 teaspoon lemon juice
1 teaspoon dried basil, crushed
⅛ teaspoon ground red pepper

• • •

Lettuce leaves

In a large bowl sprinkle gelatin over cold water to soften; let stand for 5 minutes. Add boiling broth; stir until dissolved. Let cool for 5 minutes. Whisk in mayonnaise and lemon juice. Chill mixture for 15 to 20 minutes, or until mixture is the consistency of unbeaten egg whites.

Place tuna in blender container or food processor bowl. Cover and process until pureed. Fold into gelatin mixture with cucumber and carrot. Gently fold beaten egg whites into mixture. Transfer to a 4-cup mold. Cover and chill for 4 hours or overnight until set.

For Parsley Sauce, in blender container or food processor bowl place remaining ingredients except lettuce in order listed. Cover and process until smooth. (For thinner consistency, add 1 to 2 tablespoons of milk if needed.) Unmold mousse onto lettuce-lined platter; serve with Parsley Sauce. Makes 8 appetizer or first-course servings.

Preparation time: 30 minutes
Calorie count: 165 calories per serving.

Tuna Normandy

A French classic, with apples, cream and brandy, gets a lighter twist with tuna.

3 medium Granny Smith apples, cored, peeled and thinly sliced
1 cup celery, cut diagonally into slices
⅓ cup chopped green onions
3 tablespoons butter or margarine
¾ cup apple juice
¾ cup dry white wine
1 teaspoon grated lemon peel

1½ tablespoons cornstarch
1 cup low-fat milk
1 can (12½ ounces) StarKist Tuna, drained and broken into chunks
¼ cup chopped parsley
2 tablespoons apple brandy or brandy
¼ teaspoon ground cinnamon
¼ teaspoon ground allspice
Hot cooked rice or pasta

In a large deep skillet sauté apples, celery and onions in butter for 5 minutes. Stir in apple juice, wine and lemon peel; bring to a boil. Reduce heat; simmer, uncovered, for 5 minutes, or until mixture is partially reduced. Stir cornstarch into milk until smooth; add to mixture. Return to a boil; reduce heat. Stir in tuna, parsley, brandy and spices. Cook for 2 minutes more to heat through. Serve sauce over rice. Makes 4 servings.

Preparation time: 20 minutes
Calorie count: 544 calories, including 1 cup cooked rice, per serving.

Spiral Pasta Salad

Pasta bow ties or shells are ideal for this salad too!

8 ounces tri-color spiral pasta, cooked according to package directions
1 can (12½ ounces) StarKist Tuna, drained and broken into chunks
1 cup slivered pea pods

1 cup chopped yellow squash or zucchini
1 cup asparagus, cut into 2-inch pieces
½ cup slivered red onion
½ cup sliced pitted ripe olives

Dijon Vinaigrette

⅓ cup white wine vinegar
¼ cup olive or vegetable oil
2 tablespoons water

2 teaspoons Dijon mustard
1 teaspoon dried basil, crushed
¼ teaspoon pepper

• • •

Lettuce leaves

For salad, rinse pasta in cool water; drain well. In a large bowl toss together pasta, tuna, pea pods, squash, asparagus, onion and olives. For dressing, in a shaker jar combine remaining ingredients except lettuce. Cover and shake until well blended. Pour over salad; toss well. Serve on lettuce-lined plates. Makes 5 servings.

Preparation time: 15 minutes
Calorie count: 390 calories per serving.

Easy Seafood Salad

1 can (6½ ounces) StarKist Tuna, drained and flaked
1 can (6 ounces) salmon, drained, flaked and skin and bones removed
1½ cups cooked diced potatoes
½ cup frozen peas, thawed
½ cup frozen niblet corn, thawed
⅓ cup chopped onion

¼ cup reduced-calorie mayonnaise or salad dressing
¼ cup reduced-calorie cream cheese
1 tablespoon low-fat milk
1 tablespoon tartar sauce
Salt and pepper to taste
Lettuce leaves

In a large bowl toss together tuna, salmon, potatoes, peas, corn and onion. For dressing, in a small blender container or food processor bowl combine mayonnaise, cream cheese, milk and tartar sauce. Cover and blend until smooth. Stir dressing into salad; toss well. Serve salad on lettuce-lined plates. Makes 4 to 6 servings.

Preparation time: 15 minutes
Calorie count: 348 calories per serving. (Based on 4 servings.)

Spiral Pasta Salad

Scandinavian Smörgåsbord

Use the ingredients listed below to get your imagination started; you may have other interesting tidbits or vegetables on hand to use as attractive garnishes.

36 slices party bread, crackers or
    flat bread
    Reduced-calorie mayonnaise or
    salad dressing
    Mustard
36 small lettuce leaves or Belgian
    endive leaves
1 can (6½ ounces) StarKist Tuna,
    drained and flaked or broken
    into chunks

2 hard-cooked eggs, sliced
¼ pound frozen cooked bay
    shrimp, thawed
½ medium cucumber, thinly sliced
36 pieces steamed asparagus tips
    or pea pods
    Capers, plain yogurt, dill sprigs,
    pimiento strips, red or black
    caviar, sliced green onion for
    garnish

Arrange party bread on a tray; spread each with 1 teaspoon mayonnaise and/or mustard. Top with a small lettuce leaf. Top with tuna, egg slices, shrimp, cucumber or steamed vegetables. Garnish as desired. Makes 36 appetizers.

Preparation time: 20 minutes
Calorie count: 47 calories per appetizer. Garnishes are extra.

Tuna & Wild Rice Amandine

Purchase "instant" wild rice that's been presoaked, so you can cook it whenever you need it—such as for this molded pilaf.

1 package (4 ounces) presoaked
    wild rice
    Beef broth
2 cups sliced fresh mushrooms
1 cup slivered carrots
½ cup minced onion
2 tablespoons butter or
    margarine

2 tablespoons all-purpose flour
1⅓ cups low-fat milk
1 can (9¼ ounces) StarKist Tuna,
    drained and flaked
1 cup cooked white rice
1 to 2 tablespoons dry sherry
2 tablespoons toasted slivered
    almonds

In a 2-quart saucepan cook wild rice according to package directions, except use beef broth in place of the water. In a large skillet sauté mushrooms, carrots and onion in butter for 3 to 5 minutes, or until vegetables are crisp-tender. Sprinkle flour over mixture, stirring until blended. Add milk all at once. Cook and stir until mixture thickens and bubbles. Reduce heat; stir in cooked wild rice (drained if necessary), tuna, white rice and sherry to taste. Cook for 2 to 3 minutes to heat. Pour into a 5-cup lightly greased mold; let stand for 5 minutes. Unmold onto a serving platter; sprinkle with toasted almonds. Makes 4 to 5 servings.

Preparation time: 25 minutes
Calorie count: 405 calories per serving. (Based on 4 servings.)

Scandinavian Smörgåsbord

Tuna & Zucchini-Stuffed Manicotti

Use a cookie press or pastry bag fitted with a large round tip to fill the manicotti shells easily. An iced tea spoon with a long, slender handle also works well.

1 cup diced zucchini
½ cup chopped onion
1 clove garlic, minced
1 tablespoon vegetable oil
1 can (6½ ounces) StarKist Tuna, drained and flaked
1 cup low-fat ricotta cheese

½ cup shredded mozzarella cheese
¼ cup grated Parmesan or Romano cheese
1 extra-large egg, lightly beaten
2 teaspoons dried basil, crushed
8 manicotti shells, cooked and drained

Marinara Sauce

1½ cups chopped fresh tomatoes
1¼ cups tomato sauce
2 tablespoons minced parsley
1 teaspoon dried basil, crushed

1 teaspoon dried oregano or marjoram, crushed
Salt and pepper to taste

In a medium skillet sauté zucchini, onion and garlic in oil for 3 minutes; remove from heat. Stir in tuna. In a medium bowl stir together ricotta, mozzarella, Parmesan, egg and basil until blended. Stir cheese mixture into tuna mixture; set aside.

Preheat oven to 350°F. Placed drained manicotti shells in a bowl of cold water. Set aside. For Marinara Sauce, in a medium saucepan stir together tomatoes, tomato sauce and herbs. Heat to a boil; remove from heat. Season to taste with salt and pepper. Transfer mixture to blender container or food processor bowl. Cover and process in 2 batches until nearly smooth. Spray a 13×9×2-inch baking dish with aerosol shortening.

Spread ½ cup of the Marinara Sauce over bottom of baking dish. Blot manicotti shells carefully with paper towels. Generously pipe filling into shells. In baking dish arrange manicotti in a row. Pour remaining sauce over manicotti; cover with foil. Bake for 30 minutes; uncover and bake for 5 to 10 minutes more, or until sauce is bubbly. Let stand for 5 minutes before serving. Makes 4 servings.

Preparation time: 30 minutes
Calorie count: 333 calories per serving.

Tuna & Zucchini-Stuffed Manicotti

Tuna & Shrimp Crepes Neptune

Ready-made crepes are available in packages of ten, either in the produce department or freezer case of your supermarket.

2 tablespoons butter or
   margarine
2 tablespoons all-purpose flour
1½ cups low-fat milk
¼ cup dry white wine
½ pound deveined shelled cooked
   shrimp
½ pound asparagus, cut into
   1-inch pieces and steamed

1 can (6½ ounces) StarKist Tuna,
   drained and broken into
   chunks
¼ teaspoon pepper
⅛ teaspoon ground nutmeg
⅓ cup grated Parmesan or
   Romano cheese
½ cup shredded Swiss cheese
8 ready-made crepes

Preheat oven to 375°F. In a 2-quart saucepan melt butter; stir in flour. Add milk all at once. Cook and stir until mixture thickens and bubbles. Stir in wine, shrimp, asparagus, tuna, pepper and nutmeg. Stir in Parmesan. Spray a shallow casserole with aerosol shortening. Fill each crepe with about ½ cup of the tuna mixture; arrange crepes, seam side down, in dish. Sprinkle Swiss cheese over crepes. Bake for 8 to 10 minutes, or until crepes are hot and cheese is melted. Makes 4 servings.

Preparation time: 15 minutes
Calorie count: 343 calories per serving.

Tuna & Shells Dijon

Sauce à la Moutarde, a French classic, combines Dijon mustard, cream and lemon juice. Here's a low-calorie American interpretation.

1 cup diced red, yellow or green
   bell pepper
⅓ cup chopped green onions
2 teaspoons mustard seed
2 tablespoons butter or
   margarine
2 tablespoons all-purpose flour
2½ cups low-fat milk
3 to 4 tablespoons Dijon mustard

1 teaspoon grated lemon peel
½ teaspoon salt
¼ teaspoon pepper
1 can (12½ ounces) StarKist
   Tuna, drained and flaked
1 package (7 ounces) medium
   shells, cooked and drained
2 tablespoons chopped parsley

In a medium saucepan sauté bell pepper, onions and mustard seed in butter for 3 minutes. Sprinkle flour over mixture, stirring until blended. Add milk all at once. Cook and stir until mixture thickens and bubbles. Stir in mustard, lemon peel, salt and pepper until blended. Fold in tuna and shells; cook for 2 minutes more to heat through. Serve in 4 to 6 individual casseroles or ramekins, sprinkled with parsley. Makes 4 to 6 servings.

Preparation time: 15 minutes
Calorie count: 435 calories per serving. (Based on 4 servings.)

Creole-Style Tuna

Add some red pepper sauce to this dish, to taste, for the spicier palates at your table.

1½ cups cubed peeled eggplant
  1 cup chopped onion
  1 cup cubed red or green bell pepper
  2 stalks celery, cut diagonally into slices
  2 cloves garlic, minced
  2 tablespoons vegetable oil
  1 can (28 ounces) Italian-style tomatoes with juice, cut up

1 cup chicken broth
1 can (9¼ ounces) StarKist Tuna, drained and broken into chunks
1 can (6 ounces) tomato paste
½ teaspoon dried thyme, crushed
¼ teaspoon black pepper
⅛ teaspoon ground red pepper
  Hot cooked rice

In a large saucepan or Dutch oven sauté eggplant, onion, bell pepper, celery and garlic in oil for 5 minutes. Stir in tomatoes and chicken broth; bring to a boil. Reduce heat; simmer for 10 to 15 minutes, or until vegetables are nearly tender. Stir in tuna, tomato paste, thyme, black pepper and red pepper until blended; cook for 2 minutes more, or until heated through. Serve over hot cooked rice. Makes 4 to 6 servings.

Preparation time: 20 minutes
Calorie count: 413 calories, including 1 cup cooked rice, per serving. (Based on 4 servings.)

Tuna-Stuffed Endive

4 ounces soft-spread herb cheese
4 ounces reduced-calorie cream cheese, softened
1 teaspoon lemon or lime juice
2 heads Belgian endive or small lettuce leaves or crackers

1 can (3¼ ounces) StarKist Tuna, drained and finely flaked
Watercress sprigs or pimiento strips for garnish

In a blender container or food processor bowl place cheeses and lemon juice. Cover and process until mixture is well blended. Trim ½ inch from bottom stems of Belgian endive; separate heads into leaves. Sprinkle 1 to 2 teaspoons tuna into leaves; spoon or pipe 2 teaspoons of the cheese filling over endive. Garnish each with a sprig of watercress. Makes about 24 appetizers.

Preparation time: 15 minutes
Calorie count: 29 calories per appetizer.

Tuna Salad Elegante

A round bread loaf serves as an attractive container for an asparagus-olive tuna salad.

1 round bread loaf (about 1½ pounds)
1 can (12½ ounces) StarKist Tuna, drained and flaked
6 spears cooked asparagus, trimmed and cut into 2-inch pieces

2 hard-cooked eggs, chopped
½ cup sliced pitted ripe and stuffed green olives
⅓ cup chopped green onions

Dressing

⅓ cup reduced-calorie mayonnaise or salad dressing
¼ cup plain low-fat yogurt
2 tablespoons red wine vinegar

1 teaspoon dried tarragon, crushed
1 teaspoon dried basil, crushed

• • •

Lettuce leaves

With a sharp knife, cut a 1-inch-thick slice from top of bread loaf. Reserve to use later for the lid. Then, hollow out loaf, making a 1-inch shell. If preparing ahead, wrap hollow loaf and bread top in plastic wrap. Save bread for another use.

To make salad, in a large bowl toss together tuna, asparagus, eggs, olives and onions. In a small bowl stir together mayonnaise, yogurt, vinegar, tarragon and basil. Spoon over salad; toss well to coat. If preparing ahead, cover and chill.

To serve salad, line bread shell with lettuce leaves. Spoon tuna mixture into shell. Add bread top if desired. Serve with flat crackers or party bread. Makes 3½ cups salad; about 5 to 6 main-dish or about 30 appetizer servings.

Preparation time: 30 minutes
Calorie count: 212 calories per main-dish serving (based on 5 servings); 36 calories per appetizer serving.

Tuna Calcutta

1½ cups chopped red and green
    bell pepper
½ cup sliced green onions
2 cloves garlic, minced
1 to 2 teaspoons curry powder
2 tablespoons vegetable oil
3 tablespoons all-purpose flour
2 cups low-fat milk
½ teaspoon salt
¼ teaspoon pepper

1 can (12½ ounces) StarKist
    Tuna, drained and broken
    into chunks
Hot cooked rice or pasta
Chopped cilantro, peanut
    halves, shredded coconut,
    chopped red onion and
    golden or dark raisins for
    condiments

In a large skillet sauté bell pepper, onions and garlic with curry powder in oil over medium-high heat for 3 to 4 minutes, or until vegetables are tender. Stir in flour until blended; add milk all at once. Cook and stir until mixture thickens and bubbles; cook for 2 minutes. Stir in salt and pepper; add tuna. Cook for 2 minutes more to heat through. Serve over rice; pass condiments. Makes 4 to 5 servings.

Preparation time: 20 minutes
Calorie count: 400 calories, including ¾ cup cooked rice, per serving. Condiments are extra. (Based on 4 servings.)

Tuna Continental

Here's an elegant way to enjoy tuna with friends. Surround the salad with lemon slices and small crackers or petite slices of French bread.

1 can (12½ ounces) StarKist
    Tuna, drained and flaked
½ cup finely chopped red onion
⅓ cup olive or vegetable oil
2 tablespoons white wine vinegar
2 tablespoons lemon juice
2 teaspoons drained capers

2 tablespoons chopped fresh dill
½ teaspoon salt
¼ teaspoon pepper
Lettuce leaves
Black or red caviar, fresh dill
    sprigs or lemon slices for
    garnish

In a large, nonmetal bowl toss together tuna and onion. In a medium shaker jar combine oil, vinegar, lemon juice, capers, dill, salt and pepper. Cover and shake until well blended; pour mixture over tuna and toss well. Cover and chill for 1 to 24 hours before serving to blend flavors.

To serve, spoon salad onto lettuce-lined plates; garnish with caviar, dill and lemon. Makes 2½ cups, enough for 4 main-dish or 40 appetizer servings.

Preparation time: 10 minutes
Calorie count: 284 calories per main-dish serving; 29 calories per appetizer serving.

Tuna Calcutta

Ethnic

SPECIALTIES

Tuna & Shrimp Fajitas

1 large red onion, cut in half and
  thinly sliced
1 red bell pepper, cut into bite-
  sized strips
1 large green bell pepper, cut into
  bite-sized strips
2 tablespoons vegetable oil
1 jar (12 ounces) salsa
1 can (6½ ounces) StarKist Tuna,
  drained and broken into
  chunks

½ pound frozen cooked bay
  shrimp, thawed
8 (8-inch) flour tortillas, warmed
  if desired
Diced avocado, shredded low-
  fat Cheddar or Monterey Jack
  cheese, sliced pitted ripe
  olives and bottled salsa for
  toppings

In a large skillet or wok stir-fry onion and bell peppers in oil for 3 minutes over high heat. Add ¼ cup of the salsa, the tuna and shrimp; stir-fry for 2 minutes more, or until heated through.

To assemble fajitas, spoon some of the tuna mixture in center of each tortilla, then add desired toppings and serve immediately. Makes 4 servings.

Preparation time: 10 minutes
Calorie count: 375 calories per serving. Toppings are extra.

Tuna & Shrimp Fajitas

Tortellini with Three-Cheese Tuna Sauce

1 pound cheese-filled tortellini,
   spinach and egg
2 green onions, thinly sliced
1 clove garlic, minced
1 tablespoon butter or margarine
1 cup low-fat ricotta cheese
½ cup low-fat milk
1 can (6½ ounces) StarKist Tuna,
   drained and broken into
   chunks

½ cup shredded low-fat mozzarella
   cheese
¼ cup grated Parmesan or
   Romano cheese
2 tablespoons chopped fresh basil
   or 2 teaspoons dried basil,
   crushed
1 teaspoon grated lemon peel
Fresh tomato wedges for
   garnish (optional)

Cook tortellini in boiling salted water according to package directions. When tortellini is nearly done, in another saucepan sauté onions and garlic in butter for 2 minutes. Whisk in ricotta cheese and milk. Add tuna, cheeses, basil and lemon peel. Cook over medium-low heat until mixture is heated and cheeses are melted.

Drain pasta; add to sauce. Toss well to coat; garnish with tomato wedges if desired. Serve immediately. Makes 4 to 5 servings.

Preparation time: 25 minutes
Calorie count: 550 calories per serving. (Based on 4 servings.)

Tuna Chilies Rellenos

Stuffed chilies are traditionally deep-fried, but in this recipe, the chilies are baked to keep the fat content low.

8 Anaheim or large mild green
   chilies
1 can (6½ ounces) StarKist Tuna,
   drained and flaked
1 cup shredded Monterey Jack
   cheese or pepper cheese

½ cup low-fat ricotta cheese
½ cup niblet corn, drained
1 extra-large egg
Fresh cilantro or parsley sprigs
   (optional)

Preheat oven to 425°F. Wash and dry chilies.* Cut stems from chilies; cut lengthwise into halves. Remove seeds and ribs. In a small bowl stir together tuna, cheeses, corn and egg until well mixed. Stuff each chili with about ¼ cup of the mixture. Spray a baking sheet with aerosol shortening; place stuffed chilies on baking sheet. Cover with foil. Bake for 20 to 25 minutes, or until chilies are soft and filling is heated through. Makes 4 servings; 2 chilies per serving.

*Do not touch face or eyes while handling chilies; wash hands thoroughly in soapy water after handling.

Preparation time: 10 minutes
Calorie count: 287 calories per serving.

Tortellini with Three-Cheese Tuna Sauce

Baha Roll

This Mexican takeoff on sushi features tuna in a colorful filling. Serve this as an appetizer or entrée.

1 cup uncooked quick-cooking rice
1½ cups chicken broth
¼ cup reduced-calorie mayonnaise or salad dressing
1 tablespoon rice vinegar or white wine vinegar
1 tablespoon minced green onion
2 teaspoons grated gingerroot or ¼ teaspoon ground ginger
4 (8-inch) flour tortillas
½ pound fresh spinach (1 bunch), stems removed

1 can (6½ ounces) StarKist Tuna, drained and flaked
¾ cup thin julienne-strip, peeled cucumber
¼ medium-ripe avocado, pitted, peeled and thinly sliced
1 egg white, beaten
Pickled ginger strips, thin julienne-strip carrot and fresh cilantro or parsley for garnish (optional)

Cook rice according to package directions, using chicken broth in place of water. Fluff rice; cool or cover and chill if preparing ahead. In a small bowl stir together mayonnaise, vinegar, onion and gingerroot; stir mixture into cooked rice until well combined. To assemble rolls, place tortillas on flat surface. Spread ¼ of the rice mixture evenly over each tortilla to within ½ inch of edge. Arrange spinach leaves, overlapping slightly, over rice layer. Sprinkle tuna and cucumber evenly over spinach. On each tortilla, place 2 slices of avocado crosswise over center of filling. Starting at bottom edge of each tortilla, roll up tightly, enclosing filling and avocado in center. Moisten opposite edge of tortilla with egg white; press edges together to seal. Wrap in waxed paper and twist ends; chill at least 2 hours before serving.

To serve, unwrap rolls; slice each roll crosswise into eight 1-inch slices. Garnish as desired. Makes 4 main-dish or about 32 appetizer servings.

Preparation time: 35 minutes
Calorie count: 381 calories per main-dish serving; 48 calories per appetizer.

Baha Roll

Tuna & Eggplant Parmigiana

⅓ cup chopped onion
2 cloves garlic, minced
1 tablespoon olive or vegetable oil
2 large tomatoes, chopped
1 can (8 ounces) tomato sauce
⅓ cup tomato paste
2 teaspoons dried Italian seasoning, crushed
¼ teaspoon pepper

1 can (9¼ ounces) StarKist Tuna, drained and broken into chunks
1 eggplant, peeled (about 2 pounds)
⅔ cup grated Parmesan or Romano cheese
1 cup shredded low-fat mozzarella cheese
3 tablespoons minced parsley

In a medium saucepan sauté onion and garlic in oil for 3 minutes, or until tender. Stir in tomatoes, tomato sauce, tomato paste, Italian seasoning and pepper. Bring to a boil; reduce heat. Simmer, uncovered, for 10 minutes, stirring occasionally. Stir tuna into sauce; remove from heat and set aside.

Preheat oven to 350°F. Cut eggplant crosswise into ¼-inch-thick slices. Bring a large pot of water to a boil; add eggplant. Simmer for 20 minutes, or until tender. Drain eggplant; blot dry with paper towels. In a 12×8×2-inch casserole arrange ⅓ of the eggplant; spoon ⅓ of the tomato sauce over. Sprinkle ⅓ of the Parmesan and mozzarella cheeses over top. Repeat layers twice, ending with the cheeses.

Sprinkle parsley over top. Bake, uncovered, for 25 to 30 minutes, or until hot and bubbly. Makes 6 servings.

Preparation time: 20 minutes
Calorie count: 267 calories per serving.

Tuna Salad Orientale

Ramen noodle soup mix provides the crunchy no-cook noodles for this Far-Eastern salad.

4 cups shredded iceberg lettuce
1 cup shredded red cabbage
1 can (12½ ounces) StarKist Tuna, drained and broken into chunks
½ cup bean sprouts
½ cup shredded cucumber

½ cup pea pods, stringed and cut into thin strips
½ cup shredded carrot
¼ cup chopped green onions
½ package (3 ounces) ramen noodle soup mix

Soy-Sesame Dressing

¼ cup water
3 tablespoons rice or white
    vinegar
3 tablespoons sesame oil
1 tablespoon soy sauce

1 tablespoon roasted or regular
    sesame seed
2 teaspoons sugar
¼ teaspoon pepper

In a large bowl toss together lettuce, cabbage, tuna and remaining vegetables. Remove noodles from soup mix; break noodles in half. Reserve ½ of the noodles and seasoning packet for another use. Crush remaining noodles with hands and sprinkle over salad. For Soy-Sesame Dressing, in a shaker jar combine remaining ingredients. Cover and shake until well blended. Pour over salad and toss to combine. Makes 4 servings.

Preparation time: 20 minutes
Calorie count: 320 calories per serving.

Tuna Tabbouli

This Middle-Eastern salad, flavored with mint, garlic and lemon, tastes even better the second day.

2 cups fine bulgur (cracked
    wheat) or raw brown rice,
    cooked according to package
    directions
1 medium tomato, diced
1 can (9¼ ounces) StarKist Tuna,
    drained and flaked

½ cup diced cucumber
½ cup sliced green onions
½ cup minced parsley
¼ cup chopped fresh mint or
    1 tablespoon dried mint,
    crushed

Lemon Vinaigrette Dressing

⅓ cup lemon juice
¼ cup olive or vegetable oil

1 teaspoon salt
½ teaspoon pepper

• • •

Fresh mint leaves for garnish

In a large bowl combine bulgur, tomato, tuna, cucumber, onions, parsley and chopped mint. In a shaker jar combine lemon juice, oil, salt and pepper. Cover and shake until well blended; pour over salad. Toss well to coat; cover and chill 1 to 24 hours before serving. Garnish with fresh mint. Makes 4 servings.

Preparation time: 20 minutes
Calorie count: 447 calories per serving.

Easy Paella

Paella is a delicious Spanish recipe that has seafood, rice and tomatoes.

1 medium onion, cut into halves and chopped
1 large red or green bell pepper, sliced
1 clove garlic, minced
2 tablespoons vegetable oil
1 can (16 ounces) tomatoes with juice, cut up
1 package (10 ounces) frozen artichoke hearts, cut into quarters

½ cup dry white wine
½ teaspoon dried thyme, crushed
¼ teaspoon salt
⅛ teaspoon saffron or turmeric
2 cups cooked rice
1 cup frozen peas
1 can (6½ ounces) StarKist Tuna, drained and broken into chunks
½ pound large shrimp, peeled and deveined

In a large skillet sauté onion, bell pepper and garlic in oil for 3 minutes. Stir in tomatoes with juice, artichoke hearts, wine and seasonings. Bring to a boil; reduce heat. Simmer for 10 minutes. Stir in rice, peas, tuna and shrimp. Cook for 3 to 5 minutes more, or until shrimp turns pink and mixture is heated. Makes 4 servings.

Preparation time: 30 minutes
Calorie count: 382 calories per serving.

Santa Fe Tuna Salad with Chili-Lime Dressing

Cilantro, chilies and lime juice lend this salad a southwestern flavor.

6 cups torn spinach or romaine lettuce leaves
1 cup half-slices red onion
½ cantaloupe melon or 1 ripe papaya, peeled, seeded and cut into thin half-slices

1 can (12½ ounces) StarKist Tuna, drained and broken into chunks
½ cup chopped fresh cilantro

Chili-Lime Dressing

¼ cup lime juice
¼ cup vegetable oil
2 teaspoons minced jalapeños or mild green chilies

1 clove garlic, minced
½ teaspoon salt
¼ teaspoon pepper

For salad, in a large bowl toss together spinach, onion, fruit, tuna and cilantro. For Chili-Lime Dressing, in a shaker jar combine remaining ingredients. Cover and shake until well blended. Pour over salad; toss well . Makes 4 servings.

Preparation time: 15 minutes
Calorie count: 298 calories per serving.

Easy Paella

Easy Calzone

"Calzone" is an Italian term for a filled turnover made with pizza dough.

1 can (10 ounces) refrigerated ready-to-use pizza dough
1 package (10 ounces) frozen chopped spinach, thawed
1 can (9¼ ounces) StarKist Tuna, drained and flaked
1 cup chopped tomatoes
2 cans (4 ounces each) sliced mushrooms, drained
1 cup shredded low-fat Cheddar or mozzarella cheese
1 teaspoon Italian seasoning or dried oregano, crushed
1 teaspoon dried basil, crushed
¼ teaspoon garlic powder
Vegetable oil
Cornmeal (optional)
1 can (8 ounces) pizza sauce

Preheat oven to 425°F. Unroll pizza dough onto a lightly floured board; cut crosswise into 2 equal pieces. Roll each piece of dough into a 12-inch circle.

Squeeze all liquid from spinach; chop fine. Over the bottom half of each circle of dough, sprinkle spinach, tuna, tomatoes, mushrooms, cheese and seasonings to within 1 inch of bottom edge. Fold top half of dough over filling, leaving bottom edge uncovered. Moisten bottom edge of dough with a little water, then fold bottom edge of dough over top edge, sealing with fingers or crimping with fork. Brush top of dough lightly with oil; sprinkle with cornmeal if desired. Place 2 filled calzones on ungreased baking sheet; bake for 25 to 30 minutes, or until deep golden brown. Meanwhile, in saucepan, heat pizza sauce. Cut each calzone in half crosswise to serve. Pass sauce to spoon over. Makes 4 servings.

Preparation time: 25 minutes
Calorie count: 425 calories, including ¼ cup pizza sauce, per serving.

Tuna-Fried Rice

3 tablespoons vegetable oil
2 eggs, lightly beaten
1 cup pea pods, stringed and cut crosswise into halves
½ cup chopped green onions
½ cup chopped red or green bell pepper
1 stalk celery, finely chopped
1 clove garlic, minced
3 cups cooked white or brown rice
1 can (9¼ ounces) StarKist Tuna, drained and flaked
¼ cup soy sauce
2 tablespoons dry sherry
⅛ teaspoon pepper

In a small skillet heat 1 tablespoon of the oil. Add eggs; cook and stir until scrambled. Cut eggs into shreds; set aside. In a large skillet sauté pea pods, onions, bell pepper, celery and garlic in remaining oil for 3 minutes. Stir in rice; stir-fry for 3 minutes. Stir in egg, tuna and seasoning until combined; cook for 2 minutes, or until heated. Makes 4 servings.

Preparation time: 20 minutes
Calorie count: 382 calories per serving.

Easy Calzone

Jade Salad with Sesame Vinaigrette

5 cups fresh spinach or romaine
    leaves, torn
1 can (9¼ ounces) StarKist Tuna,
    drained and broken into
    chunks

1 cup frozen cooked bay shrimp,
    thawed
¾ cup shredded cucumber
½ cup shredded red radishes

Sesame Vinaigrette

3 tablespoons rice vinegar or
    cider vinegar
2 tablespoons sesame oil
2 tablespoons vegetable oil

2 teaspoons soy sauce
2 teaspoons sesame seed
1 teaspoon sugar
    Salt and pepper to taste

In a large salad bowl toss together spinach, tuna, shrimp, cucumber and radishes.
For dressing, in a shaker jar combine vinaigrette ingredients. Cover and shake
until well blended. Drizzle over salad, toss well. Makes 4 servings.

Preparation time: 15 minutes
Calorie count: 339 calories per serving.

Seafood Wontons

*You'll find wonton skins in the refrigerated produce section or freezer case of
large supermarkets. You can freeze any unused wontons for future use.*

1 cup finely chopped bok choy or
    cabbage
1 can (3¼ ounces) StarKist Tuna,
    drained and finely flaked
⅓ cup shredded carrot
¼ cup minced green onions
1 egg, beaten
2 tablespoons soy sauce

1 tablespoon minced fresh
    gingerroot or 1 teaspoon
    ground ginger
28 to 30 wonton skins
    Vegetable oil for deep frying
    Plum sauce or soy sauce for
    dipping

In a medium bowl combine cabbage, tuna, carrot, onions, egg, soy sauce and ginger
until mixed. Position wonton skin with 1 point facing you. Spoon 1½ teaspoons of the
tuna mixture in center of skin (use a slotted spoon if filling is wet); moisten edges of
skins with water. Fold bottom corner over filling; fold side corners over first fold. Roll
remaining corner over to seal. Repeat with remaining ingredients.

In a wok or deep saucepan heat 3 inches of oil to 365°F. Fry wontons, a few at a
time, for 2 to 3 minutes, or until deep golden brown. Drain well on paper towels.
Serve hot with plum sauce. Makes 28 to 30 appetizers.

Preparation time: 30 minutes
Calorie count: 50 calories per wonton. Plum Sauce is extra.

Jade Salad with Sesame Vinaigrette

Tuna Treats FOR KIDS

Tuna 'n' Cheese Dogs

You don't have to use hot dog buns, but they make this sandwich a lot more fun!

2 hot dog buns, toasted if desired
   Butter or margarine (optional)
   Lettuce leaves
1 can (3¼ ounces) StarKist Tuna,
   drained and flaked
2 slices (1 ounce each) reduced-
   calorie American cheese, cut
   into ¼-inch squares

2 tablespoons chopped red or
   green bell pepper or celery
1 tablespoon reduced-calorie
   mayonnaise or salad dressing
2 teaspoons orange juice

1. Place each hot dog bun on a plate. Spread with butter if desired. Arrange small lettuce leaves on bottom half of each bun.

2. In a medium bowl stir together tuna, cheese and chopped bell pepper.

3. Stir in mayonnaise and orange juice until well mixed.

4. Spread tuna filling over lettuce on buns. Garnish as desired. Makes 2 sandwiches.

Preparation time: 10 minutes
Calorie count: 269 calories per serving.

Tuna 'n' Cheese Dogs

Bow Tie Tuna Salad

Bow tie pasta is a fun shape that's available in large supermarkets. Or, substitute shells, macaroni, spirals or ziti for the bow ties.

4 ounces bow tie pasta, cooked according to package directions and drained
1 cup red and green seedless grapes, cut into halves
1 can (3¼ ounces) StarKist Tuna, drained and flaked

½ cup coarsely chopped walnuts
¼ cup lemon-flavored low-fat yogurt
Lettuce leaves

1. Place the drained, cooked bow ties in a medium bowl. Add grapes, tuna and walnuts to bowl.

2. Stir lemon yogurt into the salad, mixing well to moisten salad.

3. Arrange lettuce leaves on 2 or 3 plates. Spoon salad onto lettuce, dividing evenly among the plates. (If desired, chill up to 6 hours before serving.) Makes 2 or 3 servings.

Preparation time: 15 minutes
Calorie count: 390 calories per serving. (Based on 2 servings.)

Tuna Noodle Soup

4½ cups chicken broth
½ cup thinly sliced celery
½ cup diced carrot
1 cup cooked egg noodles, bow ties, macaroni or spirals

1 can (3¼ ounces) StarKist Tuna, drained and flaked
1 tablespoon chopped parsley
1 teaspoon dried basil, crushed
⅛ teaspoon pepper

1. In a 2-quart saucepan bring chicken broth to a boil. Turn heat down and add celery and carrot.

2. Let the vegetables cook in gently bubbling broth for 10 minutes, or until they are tender.

3. Add noodles, tuna, parsley, basil and pepper to the soup.

4. Stir soup until all ingredients are well combined. Cook for 2 minutes more, or until hot. Makes 5 servings.

Preparation time: 15 minutes
Calorie count: 115 calories per serving.

Bow Tie Tuna Salad

Confetti Tuna in Celery Sticks

This also makes a great sandwich filling for pita bread.

1 can (3¼ ounces) StarKist Tuna, drained and flaked
½ cup shredded red or green cabbage
½ cup shredded carrot
¼ cup shredded yellow squash or zucchini

3 tablespoons reduced-calorie cream cheese, softened
1 tablespoon plain low-fat yogurt
½ teaspoon dried basil, crushed
Salt and pepper to taste
10 to 12 (4-inch) celery sticks, with leaves if desired

1. In a small bowl toss together tuna, cabbage, carrot and squash.

2. Stir in cream cheese, yogurt and basil. Add salt and pepper to taste.

3. With small spatula spread mixture into celery sticks. Makes 10 to 12 pieces.

Preparation time: 20 minutes
Calorie count: 32 calories per piece. (Based on 10 pieces.)

Stacked Tuna Salad with Bread "Sticks"

If you don't have a wide-mouth insulated container, use a similar-sized plastic storage container. It's a good idea to add a small bag of ice cubes to chill a noninsulated container until lunchtime.

½ cup shredded lettuce
2 slices tomato, cut into halves
1 can (3¼ ounces) StarKist Tuna, drained and broken into chunks
4 slices cucumber
½ cup shredded carrots or zucchini

2 tablespoons bottled reduced-calorie salad dressing, any flavor
2 slices pickle (optional)
1 slice bread
1 teaspoon butter or margarine

1. Rinse an insulated wide-mouth container with cold water; wipe dry. Sprinkle ½ of the lettuce in bottom of container; top with 2 half-slices tomato.

2. Add ½ of the tuna, 2 cucumber slices and ½ of the shredded carrots. Repeat layers using the same ingredients.

3. Spoon salad dressing over; top with pickle slices. Close container.

4. For Bread "Sticks," spread bread with butter; cut crosswise into halves. Stack slices buttered sides together. Cut stack lengthwise to make three long "sticks." Wrap securely in waxed paper or plastic wrap. Makes 1 serving.

Preparation time: 15 minutes
Calorie count: 262 calories per serving.

Confetti Tuna in Celery Sticks

Upside-Down Eggs in a Nest

Pimiento stars make great garnishes; let the kids cut pieces of pimiento with star-shaped canape cutters.

6 hard-cooked eggs
2 tablespoons reduced-calorie
  mayonnaise or salad dressing
2 tablespoons plain low-fat yogurt
¼ cup StarKist Tuna, flaked
¼ teaspoon dill weed
  Salt and pepper to taste

2 cups shredded lettuce
  Pimiento stars or strips, olive
  slices, cherry tomatoes,
  parsley sprigs, grape slices,
  lemon slices, carrot slices for
  garnish

1. Remove shells from eggs. With a small sharp knife cut eggs lengthwise into halves.

2. Using a teaspoon, scoop out yolks; place in a small bowl.

3. Stir in mayonnaise, yogurt, tuna and dill weed until well mixed. Season to taste with salt and pepper.

4. Sprinkle shredded lettuce on a serving plate to make a nest. Spoon filling into cavities of egg whites; place filled-side down on lettuce.

5. Garnish whites with suggested garnishes. Makes 4 to 6 servings.

Preparation time: 20 minutes
Calorie count: 182 calories per serving. Garnishes are extra. (Based on 4 servings.)

Tuna-Apple-Peanut Salad

Lettuce leaves
1 delicious or other sweet apple
1 stalk celery, thinly sliced
1 can (3¼ ounces) StarKist Tuna,
  drained and flaked

⅓ cup peanut halves
3 tablespoons reduced-calorie
  mayonnaise or salad dressing
1 to 2 tablespoons apple juice

1. Arrange lettuce leaves on 2 salad plates, covering each plate.

2. With an apple corer or small sharp knife, core apple; cut into quarters. Then cut each quarter into thin slices and arrange ½ of them on each plate.

3. Sprinkle ½ of the celery on each plate. Sprinkle ½ of the tuna and ½ of the peanuts on each plate.

4. In a small bowl stir together mayonnaise and enough apple juice to make a thin salad dressing. Drizzle the dressing over each salad. Makes 2 servings.

Preparation time: 10 minutes
Calorie count: 290 calories per serving.

Upside-Down Eggs in a Nest

Microwave
MARVELS

Tuna-Stuffed Sole with Lime Sauce

These spinach-vegetable-tuna stuffed sole fillets are served with a tangy lime sauce.

½ cup carrot cut into thin strips
½ cup zucchini or yellow squash
cut into thin strips
2 green onions, cut into thin
strips
1 can (6½ ounces) StarKist Tuna,
drained and flaked

2 tablespoons lemon juice
1 teaspoon dried basil, crushed
½ teaspoon dill weed
8 thin sole or other white fish
fillets (about 1½ pounds)
16 large fresh spinach leaves,
washed

Lime Sauce

½ cup chicken broth
2 tablespoons butter or
margarine
2 tablespoons lime juice

1 tablespoon cornstarch
¼ teaspoon pepper
Lemon or lime peel for garnish
(optional)

In a 1-quart microwavable bowl combine carrot, zucchini and onions. Cover with
waxed paper; micro-cook on High power for 2 to 3 minutes, or until nearly
tender, stirring once during cooking. Stir in tuna, lemon juice, basil and dill.
Arrange 1 sole fillet on a microwavable roasting rack or plate. Top with 2 spinach
leaves, overlapping if necessary. Spoon ⅛ of the vegetable mixture onto spinach;
roll up fillet from the short side, enclosing filling. Secure with wooden picks;
transfer to a shallow microwavable dish, filling side up. Repeat with remaining
fillets and filling.

Cover dish with vented plastic wrap. Micro-cook on High power for 8 to 11
minutes, or until fish flakes easily and center is hot, rotating dish once during
cooking. Let stand while making Lime Sauce.

For Lime Sauce, in a medium microwavable bowl combine all sauce ingredients
until well blended. Micro-cook on High power for 1 to 3 minutes, or until
thickened, stirring once. Serve fish with sauce. Makes 4 servings; 2 fillets per
serving.

Preparation time: 15 minutes
Calorie count: 222 calories, including 3 tablespoons sauce, per serving.

Tuna-Stuffed Sole with Lime Sauce

Sweet 'n' Sour Tuna with Pineapple

1½ cups red and green bell pepper chunks
2 green onions, cut into 2-inch pieces
2 teaspoons grated gingerroot
1 clove garlic, minced
1 can (12½ ounces) StarKist Tuna, drained and broken into chunks
1 can (11 ounces) mandarin oranges, drained

1 can (8¼ ounces) pineapple chunks in juice, drained; reserve juice
1 cup orange juice
2 tablespoons cornstarch
3 tablespoons catsup
2 tablespoons wine vinegar
1 tablespoon soy sauce
1 tablespoon brown sugar
Hot cooked saffron-flavored rice

In a 2-quart microwavable casserole combine bell pepper, onions, ginger and garlic. Cover loosely; micro-cook on High power for 2½ to 4 minutes, or until vegetables are tender; stir once. Stir in tuna, oranges and pineapple. Set aside.

In a microwavable bowl combine orange juice, pineapple juice and cornstarch. Stir in catsup, vinegar, soy sauce and brown sugar. Cover loosely; micro-cook on High power for 4 to 6 minutes, or until sauce thickens and bubbles; stir twice. Stir into tuna mixture. Cover loosely; micro-cook on High power for 2 to 3 minutes, or until heated; stir once. Serve over hot cooked rice. Makes 4 servings.

Preparation time: 15 minutes
Calorie count: 389 calories, including ¾ cup cooked rice, per serving.

Southern-Style Fish Cassoulet

Serve this stew with hot cooked noodles, rice or corn bread.

¼ cup chicken broth
1½ cups sliced fresh okra
1 cup sliced onion
1 can (16 ounces) whole tomatoes with juice, cut up
1 can (8 ounces) niblet corn, drained
1 can (6½ ounces) StarKist Tuna, drained and broken into chunks

1 can (6 ounces) minced clams, drained
1 can (6 ounces) tomato paste
1 cup water
½ cup dry white wine
1 teaspoon curry powder
1 teaspoon dried basil, crushed
¼ teaspoon pepper

In a 3-quart microwavable casserole combine broth, okra and onion. Cover; micro-cook on High power for 1½ minutes. Stir in remaining ingredients. Cover; micro-cook on High for 12 to 14 minutes; stir twice. Makes 4 servings.

Preparation time: 10 minutes
Calorie count: 204 calories per serving.

Sweet 'n' Sour Tuna with Pineapple

Tuna & Asparagus au Gratin

1 pound fresh asparagus
¼ cup water
¼ cup butter or margarine
3 tablespoons all-purpose flour
¼ teaspoon salt
⅛ teaspoon pepper
¾ cup low-fat milk

¼ cup dry white wine
1 can (12½ ounces) StarKist Tuna, drained and broken into chunks
3 tablespoons seasoned bread crumbs
3 tablespoons grated Parmesan

Trim asparagus; place in microwavable dish with tips toward center. Add water. Cover; micro-cook on High power 5 minutes, or until tender; rotate dish once.

In a 1-quart microwavable bowl micro-cook ½ of the butter on High power for 30 seconds, or until melted. Stir in flour, salt and pepper. Blend in milk and wine. Micro-cook on High power for 4 to 6 minutes, or until mixture thickens; stir every 2 minutes. Stir in tuna. Pour into 4 microwavable ramekins. Drain asparagus; arrange over tuna mixture. Melt remaining butter in microwavable dish on High power for 30 seconds. Drizzle over tops. Sprinkle with bread crumbs and cheese. Micro-cook on High power for 3 to 5 minutes, or until heated; rotate once. Makes 4 servings.

Preparation time: 10 minutes
Calorie count: 329 calories per serving.

Tuna Provençale on French Bread

Toasted bread or English muffins can be substituted for the French bread.

1 tablespoon butter or margarine
½ cup sliced onion
1 clove garlic, minced
1 can (16 ounces) Italian-style tomatoes with juice, cut up
1 can (9¼ ounces) StarKist Tuna, drained and broken into chunks
1 tablespoon chopped parsley

1 tablespoon lime or lemon juice
½ teaspoon dried thyme, crushed
½ teaspoon dried basil, crushed
½ cup dry white or red wine
1 tablespoon cornstarch
4 pieces (5 inches each) French bread, cut lengthwise into halves
⅓ cup sliced pitted ripe olives

In 3-quart microwavable casserole melt butter on High power for 40 seconds. Add onion and garlic. Cover; micro-cook on High power for 2 to 3 minutes, until tender. Stir in tomatoes with juice, tuna, parsley, lime juice and herbs. Combine wine and cornstarch until smooth; stir into tuna mixture. Cover; micro-cook on High power for 5 to 8 minutes, or until heated; turn dish ¼ turn twice. Let stand for 2 minutes. Serve over bread; sprinkle with olives. Makes 4 servings.

Preparation time: 10 minutes
Calorie count: 233 calories per serving.

Tuna & Asparagus au Gratin

Spinach-Noodle Casserole

Serve a shredded carrot salad and fresh fruit for dessert along with this easy-to-make main course.

1 package (10 ounces) frozen chopped spinach
2 cups low-fat ricotta cheese
¼ cup reduced-calorie mayonnaise or salad dressing
1 egg
2 teaspoons dried chives
1 teaspoon dried basil, crushed
½ teaspoon dill weed
¼ teaspoon salt
⅛ teaspoon pepper
4 ounces wide egg noodles or fusilli, cooked and drained
1 can (9¼ ounces) StarKist Tuna, drained and broken into chunks
½ cup shredded low-fat mozzarella cheese

Place opened spinach package in a shallow microwavable bowl. Micro-cook, uncovered, on High power for 4 to 6 minutes, or until thawed, turning every 2 minutes. Let stand for 2 minutes. Drain well and squeeze out excess moisture. In a blender container or food processor bowl combine spinach, ricotta, mayonnaise, egg and seasonings. Cover and process until smooth.

In a 9×9×2-inch microwavable casserole or 4 individual microwavable ramekins spread noodles. Top with tuna, then spread cheese mixture over tuna to edge of dish. Cover loosely; micro-cook on High power for 8 to 11 minutes, or until mixture is hot in center. Sprinkle mozzarella cheese over top. Let stand, covered, for 5 minutes, or until cheese is melted. Makes 4 servings.

Preparation time: 15 minutes
Calorie count: 421 calories per serving.

Tuna Chili Texas-Style

Tuna makes this chili light enough to enjoy without guilt.

1 cup red or green bell pepper cubes
½ cup chopped onion
½ cup chopped celery
1 clove garlic, minced
2 tablespoons water
1 can (28 ounces) whole tomatoes with juice, cut up
1 can (8 ounces) kidney beans, drained
1 can (6½ ounces) StarKist Tuna, drained and flaked
2 tablespoons red wine vinegar
1 to 2 tablespoons chili powder
1 teaspoon dried basil, crushed
1 teaspoon dried oregano, crushed
½ teaspoon ground cumin
Bottled hot pepper sauce to taste

In a 3-quart microwavable bowl or casserole combine bell pepper, onion, celery, garlic and water. Cover with waxed paper; micro-cook on High power for 4 to 5 minutes, or until vegetables are nearly tender. Stir in remaining ingredients except hot pepper sauce. Cover; micro-cook on High power for 15 to 17 minutes, to allow flavors to blend, stirring every 3 minutes. Season to taste with hot pepper sauce. Makes 4 servings.

Preparation time: 10 minutes
Calorie count: 206 calories per serving.

Tuna St. Jacques

Clam shells that are sold for baking Coquille St. Jacques also work very well in the microwave oven.

8 ounces fresh mushrooms, sliced
½ cup chopped red or green bell
   pepper
⅓ cup chopped green onions
1 can (12½ ounces) StarKist
   Tuna, drained and broken
   into chunks
1 tablespoon lemon or lime juice
½ teaspoon fines herbes

¼ teaspoon salt
¾ cup low-fat milk
¼ cup plain low-fat yogurt
2 tablespoons dry white wine
¼ cup all-purpose flour
½ cup croutons, crushed
2 tablespoons butter or
   margarine, melted

In a large microwavable bowl combine mushrooms, bell pepper and onions. Micro-cook on High power for 2½ to 4 minutes, or until vegetables are tender, stirring once. Stir in tuna, lemon juice, fines herbes and salt. Set aside.

In a 2-cup microwavable measure combine milk, yogurt and wine. Stir in flour until smooth. Micro-cook on High power for 1 to 3 minutes, or until mixture thickens and bubbles, stirring once. Stir sauce into tuna mixture, combining well. Spoon into 4 lightly greased individual microwavable baking dishes or 8 clam shells. Sprinkle crushed croutons over tops; drizzle butter over croutons. Cover loosely; micro-cook on High power for 3 to 6 minutes, or until heated through, rearranging dishes once. Makes 4 servings.

Preparation time: 15 minutes
Calorie count: 266 calories per serving.

Spaghetti Squash with Tuna-Vegetable Sauce

1 spaghetti squash (about
    1 pound), cut lengthwise into
    halves
¼ cup water
1 medium zucchini, cut
    lengthwise into quarters and
    thinly sliced
1 cup chopped carrots
½ cup chopped onion
1 clove garlic, minced

1 large fresh tomato, chopped
2 cups tomato sauce
1 can (12½ ounces) StarKist
    Tuna, drained and broken
    into chunks
1 teaspoon dried basil, crushed
1 teaspoon dried rosemary,
    crushed
¼ cup grated Parmesan or
    Romano cheese

Arrange squash, cut side up, in a shallow microwavable dish; add water. Cover loosely; micro-cook on High power for 9 to 12 minutes, rotating dish once during cooking. Let stand, covered, while preparing sauce.

In a large microwavable bowl combine zucchini, carrots, onion and garlic. Micro-cook on High power for 3 to 5 minutes, or until tender, stirring once. Stir in tomato, tomato sauce, tuna, basil and rosemary. Cover loosely; micro-cook on High power for 3 to 5 minutes, or until sauce is heated through, stirring once. Using 2 forks, remove squash pulp by pulling it from the rind. Pile it onto a serving platter. Spoon tuna sauce over; sprinkle with cheese. Garnish with fresh basil if desired. Serve immediately. Makes 4 to 5 servings.

Preparation time: 15 minutes
Calorie count: 281 calories per serving. (Based on 5 servings.)

Ziti & Tuna Bake

Here's a quick supper dish you can pull right from your pantry.

6 ounces ziti pasta, cooked and
    drained
1 jar (15 ounces) spaghetti sauce
    with mushrooms
1 can (9¼ ounces) StarKist Tuna,
    drained and broken into
    chunks

½ cup sliced pitted ripe olives
1 cup shredded low-fat mozzarella
    cheese
Chopped parsley

In a large bowl toss together cooked pasta, spaghetti sauce, tuna, olives and ½ of the mozzarella. Transfer mixture to a 10×6×2-inch microwavable casserole. Cover with waxed paper; micro-cook on High power for 9 minutes, rotating dish ¼ turn every 3 minutes. Sprinkle remaining cheese over casserole. Let stand, covered, for 2 minutes to melt cheese. Sprinkle with parsley. Makes 4 servings.

Preparation time: 20 minutes
Calorie count: 385 calories per serving.

Spaghetti Squash with Tuna-Vegetable Sauce

Tuna-Stuffed Bakers

Use your favorite in-season vegetables for the filling.

4 large baking potatoes or sweet
   potatoes, scrubbed
2 cups chopped or sliced fresh or
   frozen vegetables*
¼ cup chopped green onions
1 can (12½ ounces) StarKist
   Tuna, drained and flaked
⅓ cup low-fat ricotta cheese
2 tablespoons drained pimiento
   strips

1 tablespoon chopped parsley
   (optional)
¼ teaspoon dry mustard
⅛ teaspoon pepper
4 slices (1 ounce each) reduced-
   calorie American cheese, cut
   into ¼-inch strips

Pierce potatoes twice with fork. Arrange potatoes 1 inch apart on paper towel in microwave oven. Micro-cook on High power for 10½ to 12½ minutes, turning and rearranging potatoes halfway through cooking time. Wrap potatoes in foil; let stand for 5 minutes to finish cooking while preparing filling.

For filling, in a 2-quart microwavable casserole place desired vegetables and onions. Cover with waxed paper; micro-cook on High power for 3 to 5 minutes, or until vegetables are crisp-tender, stirring twice. Drain. Stir in tuna, ricotta cheese, pimiento, parsley, mustard and pepper until well combined. Cover; micro-cook on High power for 2 minutes, or until mixture is heated through, stirring once.

Unwrap potatoes; cut lengthwise into halves. Flake interior with fork. Spoon vegetable filling mixture over potatoes, mounding filling on top. Place potatoes in a shallow microwavable dish. Place strips of cheese diagonally over filling. Micro-cook on High power for 1 to 2 minutes, or until cheese is melted. Makes 4 servings; 2 halves per serving.

*Suggested vegetables are: broccoli or cauliflower florets, mushrooms, carrots, pea pods, peas, asparagus or corn.

Preparation time: 20 minutes
Calorie count: 358 calories per serving.

Tuna-Stuffed Bakers

California-Style Tuna Melt

This sandwich makes a superb quick lunch.

4 slices bread, 8 thin slices
    French bread or 4 (8-inch)
    flour tortillas, cut diagonally
    into halves
¼ cup reduced-calorie mayonnaise
    or salad dressing
8 thin slices tomato
1 can (9¼ ounces) StarKist Tuna,
    drained and flaked

½ cup chopped red onion
    Alfalfa sprouts
1 cup shredded low-fat Cheddar
    cheese
½ ripe avocado, peeled, pitted and
    thinly sliced

Toast bread if desired. Arrange pieces on a flat microwavable plate or tray. Spread with mayonnaise. Place 1 tomato slice on each bread half. Top with tuna, onion and some alfalfa sprouts, dividing evenly. Sprinkle cheese over bread. Cover with waxed paper. Micro-cook on High power for 2 to 4 minutes, or until sandwiches are heated through and cheese is melted, rotating dish once during cooking. Serve topped with avocado slices. Garnish as desired. Makes 4 sandwiches.

Preparation time: 15 minutes
Calorie count: 377 calories per serving with bread; 442 calories per serving with tortilla.

Tuna & Rice à la Orange

Use whatever fresh fruit is in season to complement the orange-flavored sauce.

1 cup chicken broth
½ cup orange juice
2 tablespoons cornstarch
2 strips orange peel
⅛ teaspoon pepper
⅛ teaspoon ground allspice
1 can (11 ounces) mandarin
    oranges, drained

1 can (9¼ ounces) StarKist Tuna,
    drained and broken into
    chunks
1 cup chopped fruit*
1 tablespoon chopped parsley
    Hot cooked rice

In a 2-quart microwavable casserole stir together chicken broth, juice, cornstarch, orange peel, pepper and allspice until smooth. Cover loosely; micro-cook on High power for 4 to 5 minutes, or until thickened, stirring every 2 minutes. Stir in oranges, tuna, desired fruit and parsley. Micro-cook on High power for 2 to 3 minutes more, or until heated through. Remove orange peel strips; serve over rice. Makes 4 servings.

*Suggested fruits are: peaches, melon, pineapple or halved seedless grapes.

Preparation time: 15 minutes
Calorie count: 367 calories, including 1 cup cooked rice, per serving.

California-Style Tuna Melt

Index